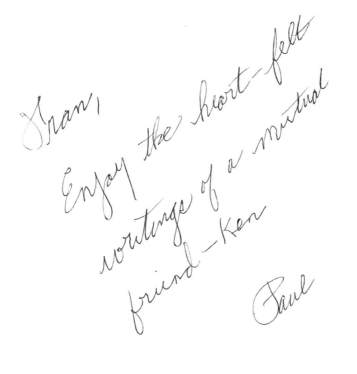

Fran,

Enjoy the heart-felt
writings of a mutual
friend — Ken

Paul

Gazing into God's Open Heart

101 Pathways to Joy

by

Kenneth E. Grabner, C.S.C.

authorHOUSE®

AuthorHouse™
1663 Liberty Drive, Suite 200
Bloomington, IN 47403
www.authorhouse.com
Phone: 1-800-839-8640

First published by AuthorHouse 1/24/2009

ISBN: 978-1-4389-1339-1 (sc)

Printed in the United States of America
Bloomington, Indiana

This book is printed on acid-free paper.

The bible text used in this publication is from the Good News Bible, Today's English Version. *Copyright American Bible Society 1976.*

TABLE OF CONTENTS

INTRODUCTION

When we open our hearts completely to someone, we reveal to that person who we really are. The revelation is a gift of intimacy that enriches the one who receives it, and so it is a cause for joy.

God, in his love, has opened his heart to us through the message and actions of Jesus, and he has revealed to us who he is. This gift of intimacy is meant to enrich us and to be the cause of our joy. Joy is Jesus' intention for all of us, for he tells us that he has spoken to us so that our joy may be full (John 15:11). Joy is what we can hope to receive when we gaze into God's open heart, and prayerfully reflect on what Jesus has revealed to us.

Not only Jesus' words, but also the entire biblical message reveals to us what is in God's heart. We can find a multitude of ways to joy through the personal application of the Bible's message to our lives. This book uses the term "101 ways to joy" to emphasize this idea. If we pay attention to our lives in the light of what the Bible tells us, we come to notice an overflowing sense of peaceful delight growing within ourselves. The 101 ways to joy are embedded in Jesus' life, words, and actions, and in all the good words and actions recorded in the Bible as a whole. Joy is God's gift to those who seek to understand these words and actions, and to live by them.

We sometimes use the number "101" to express another kind of fullness when we say, "This is going to be a busy day. I've got a 101 things to do." This can be the number's negative side. Sometimes we are bogged down with too many responsibilities, too much to accomplish. And since many of us are very busy people, each of the book's 101 ways to joy can be read in just a few short minutes. This allows time for a few moments of reflection after the brief reading. Personal reflection is vital, because it enables the reader to make the words a part of his or her life. Without personal reflection, the words will be quickly forgotten, and they won't have much influence on one's daily life. Ultimately, the revelation of an open heart can only be fully understood when it is contemplated in an admiring gaze of silence.

This book is meant to be an antidote for much of the bad news that bombards us through our newspapers and television channels. Bad news is of course an unfortunate part of life, and if we get too much of it, our view of life can become distorted. The message and actions of Jesus and the entire revelation of the Bible remind us that there is another side to life, one that reflects beauty, love, and peace. The more this message becomes embedded in our minds and hearts, the more we come to know the joy that Jesus wills us to have.

The index at the end of the book allows the reader to look for a particular topic that might meet the needs of a given moment. The message that emanates from God's open heart invites us to experience a whole range of possibilities such as hope, love, faith, perseverance, and forgiveness, to name just a few. There will be times when we will look for extra help in any one of these areas. The index can lead us to what we need most at any particular time.

Joy is meant to be the distinguishing mark of a follower of Jesus. It can be helpful to remind ourselves why this is so. God's revelation offers many examples for our reflection. May its message light a warm, gentle fire in your heart.

1.

YOU WILL ALWAYS BE COVERED WITH GOD'S LOVE.

"And I will be with you always, to the end of the age."
Mt. 28:20

These words offer the delightful promise of security and protection in our daily lives. The promise means to me that I am not alone when it comes to making difficult decisions or working through the dilemmas of my life. If I remember this promise of Jesus, I will ask for his help, especially when it seems clear that my own efforts will not be enough. Belief in this promise brings a sense of relief because it tells me that God's help and concern will always be woven into my life. If I believe that I will always be covered by a mantel of God's concern, the promise of Jesus will give birth to a feeling of joy.

Jesus promises to be with us in all that we do. I think one of the ways we experience his presence is through the inspirations we receive as a result of prayer. Where do you feel the need for inspiration and direction in your life? Parents tell me they need these things when they talk with their children. Friends need them when disagreements threaten to pull their friendships apart. I find that I need plenty of inspiration and direction when preparing homilies that I hope will be meaningful to others. I have learned never to give a homily without asking God to direct my efforts. And I can always count on God's help as long as I have done my part to the best of my ability.

Sometimes though, even with prayer, things do not turn out according to our hopes and expectations. How do we experience God's presence with us then? Is it true that God's love can manifest itself even in the midst of our misfortunes?

On a cold, snowy February day, a woman slipped on the ice and broke her ankle as she was getting into her car. Quite naturally she

1

considered this to be a tragedy, especially since there were so many things she had to do. But after a month of enforced rest and quiet, she told her friends that breaking her ankle had a positive side. For the first time in many years, she had an opportunity to slow down and reflect on how she had been living her life. And she began to realize that she had been too busy to appreciate the important gifts of life. She gave herself insufficient time to taste the peace that comes through prayer, and the joy that comes through friendships. Her time of recovery taught her that she had not been living a full life, and she decided to rearrange some of her priorities. This new direction began as a result of her broken ankle. God helped her to bring the best out of a situation that was tragic. If his promise to be with us always is true, then this is something that we can expect when misfortune strikes our lives.

How differently would you feel about your life if you realized more fully that God's presence was always with you?

2.

GOD'S FORGIVENESS IS AS CLOSE TO YOU AS YOUR BREATH.

Jesus said, "Forgive them, Father! They don't know what they are doing."

Luke 23:34

Jesus is dying on the cross in unimaginable pain, and it might seem that this is a strange time for him to be thinking of forgiveness. Yet those who are causing this horror are forgiven. They continue to be unconditionally loved. And that is the attitude that God consistently maintains toward us, because as St. John says, "God is love." (1 John 4:8). God is not able to change who he is. Unlike us, whose love can come and go, God's love always remains the same. That is simply God's nature.

This means that love and forgiveness shine out from God just as light shines out from the sun. We can shut our eyes to the light, but we can't stop it from shining. Here is the wonderful truth about God that brings us security and peace.

I have met people who have a problem with this. They feel that sometimes they are not worthy to be forgiven. But our worthiness doesn't come from our feelings about it. Worthiness comes from God's decision to love us at all times, no matter what. So we have a choice. We can hang on to guilt, or we can take God as God is and accept the forgiveness that is constantly given to us. The forgiveness will be there even if we don't accept it. But we can't be changed by God's forgiveness unless we allow it into our minds and hearts.

There's an old saying that says, "If it sounds too good to be true, it probably is." That's wise to remember when we're bombarded by advertisements that seem to promise more than they intend to deliver. But the saying is absolutely false when it comes to the promises of God.

No matter how incredible they may seem, they are always true. We are perpetually and unconditionally loved and forgiven. That may not always make sense to us, but it makes perfect sense to God. And that's really all that matters.

Are you grateful for the unconditional love and forgiveness that you have received?

3.

SOMETIMES IT'S MORE IMPORTANT TO RECEIVE THAN IT IS TO GIVE.

"You did not choose me; I chose you and appointed you to go and bear much fruit, the kind of fruit that endures."
John 15:16

All love starts with God. We have to be chosen before we can choose. We have to receive before we can give.

It might seem selfish to think that receiving is more important than giving. Doesn't that fly in the face of what we were taught? When it is a question of our relationships with one another, then it might seem more altruistic to give than to receive. But when it is a question of our relationship to God, then it is far better to receive than to give. For if we don't first receive, and continue to receive, then we have nothing to give. Everything starts with God, and so whatever we have ultimately comes from him as a free gift of his love. If we want to live a truthful life, it is important for us to recognize our dependence on God for all that we have and to be grateful receivers.

If we happen to be somewhat unaware of how our lives really work, it can be a temptation to suppose that we alone are mainly responsible for our achievements. This reminds me of the first time I ever drove a car. I was three years old. My dad stopped the Plymouth just outside of the garage, put me on his lap, placed my hands on the steering wheel, and told me that I was going to drive the car into the garage. I was so excited by the experience that I didn't notice his hands on the bottom of the steering wheel. I actually thought that I was steering the car into the garage.

Of course we have much more control over our lives now than I did when steering the car in the garage at the age of three. But there is some degree of truth in the analogy. Our hands are never the only ones on the steering wheel. We were loved by God into existence long before we were able to love back in return. God touches us with his word and with the inspirations of his Spirit often in our lives. His guidance is with us, providing the force that brings some measure of success to our lives. His power gives us the possibility to achieve what we could never do if left to ourselves. This seems to be a basic message of the gospel, a message that many people tell me they come to experience as their spirituality evolves. Knowing that God's hands are with ours on the steering wheels of our lives, we find yet another basic reason for joy.

Our success in life comes through God's power, and it is sustained by his love. We receive it as a gift. Is this how you see your life?

4.
GOD ENJOYS FINDING WHAT IS LOST.

"Or suppose a woman who has ten silver coins loses one of them—what does she do? She lights a lamp, sweeps her house, and looks carefully everywhere until she finds it. When she finds it, she calls her friends and neighbors together, and says to them, 'I am so happy I found the coin I lost. Let us celebrate!'"

Luke 15:8-10

People only look for lost things if they find those things to be worthwhile. If God had not found us worthwhile, he would never have bothered looking for us. He would not have been interested, and we would simply have remained lost.

Some years ago I made a retreat at a Trappist monastery, and the guest master gave us about a seven-minute reflection at the end of each day. After all this time, I have forgotten most of what he had to say, but one idea always stuck with me. One evening he said, "Always remember that God is interested in you." That meant so much more to me than the usual phrase, "God loves you," probably because the word *love* has become trite and seems to have lost so much of its meaning. But to say "God is interested in you" is a fresh way of conveying the idea that we mean a great deal to God. It tells us that we are worthwhile to God and that he will do anything to ensure that our relationship lasts and grows. And if we wander away, God will pursue us until the relationship resumes, even if that means the giving of his life.

I could never understand just why God finds me interesting, but it is a tremendous joy for me to know that he does. This part of the gospel message tells us all that we have an unfathomable worth, and that there is nothing we can do to change God's mind about that. Of course, we can choose to remain lost, but that choice does nothing to dampen the ardor of God's unending pursuit of us.

The unfortunate result of free will is that we have the power to resist God's love. Here you have one of the major paradoxes of life. We, with our puny abilities, are able to thwart the plan of God, whose loving power created the entire universe. But that is the price God is willing to pay for our love. Our gift of a loving response to God can never be coerced if it is to be a free gift. And if it is not free, it can't really be a gift of love.

God gives us the beautiful power of freedom, and in our finer moments we use it well. We freely choose to make a response to God, who invites us to the fullness of intimacy. When we respond, our lives have meaning. When we don't respond, there is still hope, because the divine hunter pursues us as his most precious prey. He never gives up, and we experience our greatest joy when we allow his pursuit to succeed.

What a great sense of security we have in knowing that God never gets tired of searching for us. How many times have you been lost and found?

5.

It pays to give thanks.

Jesus spoke up, "There were ten men who were healed; where are the other nine?"

Luke 17:17

That was Jesus' question when only one of the ten lepers who were healed returned to give him thanks. The other nine disappointed Jesus by their lack of gratitude, but they also impoverished themselves by their failure to return and give thanks. We need to consider why this was so, because there may be times when our own lack of gratitude impoverishes us. We can also look at the other side of the coin. We can consider those times when we were enriched by our gratitude toward God and toward all those who were good to us.

A friend of mine recently bought a new computer for me, and this was a replacement for a computer that he had bought about six years previously. The use of these computers brought a tremendous amount of enjoyment by giving me the ability to do things I otherwise would not have been able to do. But beyond the enjoyment of the computers, there was the joy of realizing how much my friend cared about me. That would have been missing had I not felt gratitude for his kindness. If I had not appreciated his generosity, I would not have fully appreciated him or the significance of his friendship. This would have been a case of getting lost in the gift and forgetting the giver. A great way to rob yourself of a sense of joy!

None of this is meant to suggest that a friendship is good only if you get something material out of it. But when a gift comes your way, it pays to give thanks. Gratitude deepens your relationship to the giver. The leper who returned to give thanks had a deeper appreciation of Jesus than did the other nine.

We are all blessed throughout our lives with many gifts, not only from God, but also from others who love us. It brings us joy when we take time to remember to be thankful for them. When we are grateful, we recognize what has been done for us, and we realize how much we are loved. Perhaps this is why the gospel so often stresses the importance of being thankful.

Have you ever been so lost in a gift that you forgot the giver?

6.

GOD LOVES ENTHUSIASTIC PEOPLE.

"I came to set the earth on fire, and how I wish it were already kindled!"

Luke 12:49

A careful reading of the gospel reveals a sense of urgency that permeated Jesus' preaching. What he wanted to share was so vital that it consumed all of his energy. No half-hearted efforts! No divided loyalties! The fire was within him, and he wanted to enkindle that fire in all who followed him. To be on fire for God is the most satisfying experience we can know. It brings energy to our love and to all that we do.

What would our lives be like if the fire of God were enkindled within us? There is a beautiful story about a mother who scrubbed offices at night so that her son could go to medical school. Eventually, thanks to her help, her son graduated and became a well-known physician. What went through that mother's mind as she scrubbed her nights away, week after week, month after month? What induced her to sacrifice a significant part of her life for the sake of her son's future? It was the fire, the fire within her that became a burning conviction that she was doing something meaningful for someone she loved. Even though the work may have been hard, I would guess that her motive for doing it brought her a sense of joy.

Perhaps one of the major questions Jesus addresses to us is this: "Are you catching the fire?" The fire would be more than a superficial feeling of enthusiasm. Feelings come and go. Rather, the fire would be a deep unshakeable belief that Jesus' words can transform us and bring meaning to our lives. We would be captivated by those words because they lead to the experience of Jesus in our minds and hearts.

Those who pray and try to live the gospel are the ones who catch its fire. They love more deeply, hope more confidently, and live more meaningfully because they come to know and serve Jesus. Serve the Lord with love. Serve others with love. Pray so that you can become intimate with the presence of God within you. Then Jesus' wish for you will gradually be realized. The fire will be kindled.

Have you caught the fire?

7.

GOD DOES A LOT WITH THE LITTLE WE HAVE.

"All we have here are five loaves and two fish," they replied.

Mt. 14:17

A large, hungry crowd needed to be fed, but what Jesus' disciples found would hardly have put a dent in the crowd's hunger. Just five loaves and two fish! And yet, the little they found became enough to feed more than five thousand people. There were even enough left-overs to fill twelve baskets. Jesus accomplished a marvel that was way out of proportion to the little he was given, and this was only the beginning of what he was yet to do. He did even more with the lives of his apostles.

The apostles Jesus picked to spread his message are portrayed in Scripture as sometimes lacking in faith and courage, and they failed to grasp his central message of resurrection. Perhaps one could say that they brought little to the task Jesus called them to do. And yet he took what they had and accomplished marvels with what he was given. Through the power of Jesus, the apostles grew in faith and courage. Their enthusiasm for the gospel enabled them to spread its message to thousands, and most of the apostles witnessed to it at the cost of their lives. Just as with the loaves and fish, Jesus accomplished a lot with a little.

There is an important message here for me. It seems that I too do not bring very much to the tasks that Jesus asks me to do. No great talents, no extraordinary abilities. And yet he takes the little I have and uses it to accomplish more than I would have imagined to be possible. I, who have always been somewhat shy, have been given the ability to stand up in front of others and to speak about the gospel. I can say that something similar has happened in all of the various ministries that God has called me to do. He has always done a lot with a little, and my belief that he will continue to do that brings me a lot of joy. Can we say that this is what Jesus does for all of us? Consider the following story.

A group of recovering alcoholics wanted to start a club and a halfway house in a city where none of these facilities was available. They had very little money and little expertise for organizing such an ambitious venture. Yet within five years the club, along with two halfway houses, were in full operation, serving the needs of more people than the founders would have thought possible. Truly this was God's work. He did a lot with the little that was given.

God always does a lot with a little. Can you see how he has done this in your life?

8.

YOU ARE NEVER LEFT TO FEND FOR YOURSELF.

"I am the vine, and you are the branches. Whoever remains in me, and I in him, will bear much fruit; for you can do nothing without me."

John 15:5.

Some time ago a friend of mine asked me to celebrate her wedding Mass and witness the exchange of her wedding vows. Both she and her fiancé were very deeply spiritual people, and so it was no surprise to see her fiancé kneeling in front of the tabernacle before the beginning of Mass. The idea came to me, though, that if he were having second thoughts and looking for guidance, perhaps it was a bit late. But second thoughts were furthest from his mind. He simply wanted God's love to be the bond that cemented his marriage relationship. He and his bride were to be branches that were firmly embedded into God's loving presence. That presence would be the source of the marriage's fruitfulness.

They have remained faithful, supported by their mutual love, but also by their understanding that they are branches in the vine. Difficult times were a part of their lives, just as they are a part of all lives, but this couple knew they would not have to fend for themselves. Faith in Jesus' words gave them the strength they needed to navigate through the hardships when they came. But most of all, those words were a source of joy.

If we are branches in the vine, we are never left to fend for ourselves, because we allow the power of God to flow through us. This works for us as long as we remember that we really are branches in the vine. When we recognize that and prayerfully ask for God's power to enliven us, we have a clearer understanding of who we really are.

Do you recognize who you are?

9.
LOVE GIVES BIRTH TO REPENTANCE AND FORGIVENESS.

"But whoever has been forgiven little shows only a little love."

Luke 7:47

Where there is much love, there can be much forgiveness. That is because when you have love, you have an awareness of the need for forgiveness. How does this work?

In Luke 7, the story is told about Simon, the Pharisee who invited Jesus to dinner. We don't know what his motives were, but he showed Jesus great disrespect. In the culture of that time, if you loved and respected your guest, you had someone there to wash his feet. You also greeted him with a kiss and anointed his head with oil. Simon did none of these things. To understand Simon's lack of caring, you could make a comparison to our contemporary culture. If you invited someone to dinner and tossed him a can of sardines and a stale roll and said, "Enjoy," the lack of caring would be equivalent to what Simon showed Jesus. Simon wasn't sorry about the disrespect, because he didn't really care about Jesus. Since there was no love, Simon didn't even think to ask for forgiveness. He felt no need for it.

In the midst of Simon's dinner gathering, a woman came in whose mentality was quite different from Simon's. Because she loved God, she was aware of having offended him. She supplied the gestures that Simon had omitted and asked to be forgiven for her sins. Love made her aware of her need for forgiveness, and she received it. Without the love, she would not have been much different from Simon the Pharisee.

Where does that leave us? Here is one example. If you love God, you'll ask for forgiveness for those times when you were negligent in your prayer life. If you love God, you would eventually become aware of this negligence, and it would disturb you. For if you love, you communicate with the one you love. And for the same reason, you would express regret if you spent insufficient time with your family or with those who need you.

Love invites us to see where we need to repent. That is what leads us back to where we should be with God and with others. If we love much, we will regret our offenses against those we love. That is what opens our hearts to God's forgiveness.

Do you have enough love to recognize your need for forgiveness?

10.

TREASURE WHAT IS GOOD IN YOUR LIFE.

So Jesus went back with them to Nazareth, where he was obedient to them. His mother treasured all these things in her heart.

Luke 2:51

Mary cherished her memories of Jesus, because love would have it no other way. We can suppose that Joseph, along with Mary's relatives and friends, found their places in her memory too. The cherishing of memories added beauty to her life, and it seems that there is a message here for us. We have our own memories to cherish. Being attentive to them helps us to appreciate the many gifts that have been a part of our lives. That can bring much joy.

I cherish the memory of my parents and remember all that they have meant to me throughout my life. Much of what I have been able to do has been built on the foundation of love and guidance they provided for me when I was young. I remember my relatives and friends whose goodness has enriched my life. With gratitude, I remember many of my teachers. Without them, I would not have acquired the skills that helped me accomplish what I have been asked to do. Then there is the gift of health, and the many opportunities to serve others. I remember these too as part of the gift of life. There is, of course, so much more. The more aware I am of all of these gifts, the more appreciative I am for the gift of life. Mary's attitude prompts me to keep remembering.

Of course, not all of our memories are good or enjoyable. Mary had to remember the flight into Egypt, the brief disappearance of Jesus in Jerusalem when he was twelve, and the horrors of his passion and death. We have our own painful memories: premature deaths of people we loved, different kinds of failure, and hurtful betrayals. Some of these may entail the need to forgive ourselves or to forgive others so that we can be set free. And there may be times when we will need others to help us in this process.

Do you remember with gratitude the blessings of your life? Do you enjoy the freedom of having forgiven those who have hurt you?

11.

LISTEN TO YOUR MESSENGERS.

The angel said to her, "Don't be afraid, Mary; God has been gracious to you. You will become pregnant and give birth to a son, and you will name him Jesus. He will be great and will be called the Son of the Most High God."

Luke 1:30-32

Mary accepted this messenger and his message, and that changed not only her life, but ours as well. How different things would have been for her and for us had she met the message with a refusal. This holds true for the other messages of the gospel too.

Joseph received a message not to be afraid to take Mary as his wife, and he obeyed. It was a decision that radically changed his life. Zechariah received a message that his wife Elizabeth was to bear a child in her old age, but Zechariah doubted. As a result, he was unable to speak until shortly before the birth of his son, John the Baptist. Often, messages in the gospel were given through the activity of angels, and we can certainly consider the apostles to have been messengers of Jesus. The gospel shows us that paying attention to messengers was important if a person were to be fully open to the word of God.

In our day, we may not receive messages through angels, but we do receive them often through the words, actions, and writings of others. When I was a teenager, I felt a strong attraction to the religious life, but I was confused as to where I should go. The messenger came to me in the form of a booklet put out by a Cistercian monastery in Wisconsin. I remember digging through a huge box containing dozens of booklets advertising various religious communities, but when I saw the Cistercian booklet, I knew almost immediately that was where God wanted me to go. The booklet was my messenger. Throughout my life, various people and various books have been messengers, each coming at a time in my spiritual life when they were needed. They gave new insights to me, and I can't imagine my life without these messengers. If I hadn't recognized them and listened, much richness in my life would have been lost.

The gospel reveals the importance of paying attention to our messengers and their messages. There may be more of them than we think. We need to be aware of them and to see their importance as they come to us in the everyday circumstances of our lives.

Are you aware of the messengers that come to you in your daily life?

12.

FIND TRUTH IN YOUR WEAKNESS.

Then Peter spoke up. "Lord, if it is really you, order me to come out on the water to you." "Come!" answered Jesus. So Peter got out of the boat and started walking on the water to Jesus. But when he noticed the strong wind, he was afraid and started to sink down in the water. "Save me, Lord!" he cried.

Mt. 14:28-30

Jesus saved Peter, but not without forcing him to face his fear and lack of faith. This was the truth Peter had to come to terms with. On the night that began Jesus' passion and death, Peter failed once again when, out of fear, he denied knowing Jesus. Perhaps most of us would have acted just as Peter did. Fear and lack of faith feed upon each other, and when the chips are down, they often show up to make our lives miserable. Finally we discover that we can't deal with them by ourselves. We have to let God take over. That is the truth that finally sets us free and brings us joy.

Peter did overcome his fear and lack of faith. He endured hardships as he preached the gospel of Jesus and underwent martyrdom courageously for the sake of this gospel. That is what the grace of God enabled him to do. And that same grace strengthens our faith and enables us to do what we have to in spite of our fears.

Perhaps today you are facing difficulties that arouse your fear and challenge your faith. If there are no difficulties now, they will eventually come, because they are an inescapable part of life. The good news is that you have God's power within you to help you deal with them. Jesus tells us this often in the gospel, and if we have faith in his words, we can find security in our daily lives.

Our faith enables us to allow God's power to work within us. The stronger the faith, the greater the ability to be open to the power God wants to give us. Pray for this faith.

Do you pray for the gift of faith, especially on those days when you need it the most?

13.

LEARNING FROM ANIMALS AND FLOWERS.

"Look at the birds: They do not plant seeds, gather a harvest, and put it into barns; yet your Father in heaven takes care of them! Aren't you worth much more than birds?"

Matt. 6:26

Jesus showed a wonderful sensitivity to his environment. He used it to teach us something about life, about our relationship to God. If God takes care of the birds, won't he take care of us? In the verses that follow Matt. 6:26, he uses the example of the flowers of the field to say the same thing. If they are so magnificently clothed with beautiful color, won't God also take care of us? In other parts of the gospel, he draws lessons from the fig tree (Mk 13:28) and from the blowing of the wind (Luke 12:55). Perhaps he would want us to do the same.

The message is not only that nature is wonderful and beautiful, but also that it reveals truths about life in a poetic way. How would our own understanding of life be deepened if we decided to be creative in our use of nature as Jesus was?

Some time ago I watched a heron standing motionless along the shore of a pond, waiting for its fish dinner to swim into view. Minute after minute passed by, and it seemed as if this bird was never going to get what it was so patiently waiting for. But just as I was about to turn away, the heron plunged into the water and returned with its prey. He got the fish not only because of a built-in fishing expertise that was a part of its nature, but also because of the patience that enabled it to wait endlessly for the fish.

This wonderful scenario reflected an important lesson to me, because patience is not one of my chief virtues. I want projects to be accomplished faster than they can be, red lights to turn green before their time, and Indiana winters to end in February. Of course all that this attitude does is to create stress, which robs me of the efficiency I need to do things well. The heron, on the other hand, seemed majestically serene, and its patience resulted in a tasty reward. Here was something to think about.

Flowers can teach us something too. One day as I was driving along a street that contained a small island filled with chunks of concrete and various forms of trash, I noticed a lone black-eyed Susan waving her bloom above the debris. Since I was stopped by a red light, I had time to reflect on this unusual sight. Here was one lone flower that managed to bloom in a most ugly and unlikely place. And the thought occurred to me: If a flower could do that, then couldn't I do the same when the circumstances of my life were unfavorable? That's the treasure the black-eyed Susan had for me, and I remain grateful to her.

There are many other examples of what we can learn from nature if we allow our minds to be creative. Jesus pointed out the way. A great deal of knowledge and enrichment can be ours if we follow.

Are you creative enough to see what nature has to teach you?

14.

ACCEPTING CHANGE.

Every year the parents of Jesus went to Jerusalem for the Passover Festival. When Jesus was twelve years old, they went to the festival as usual. When the festival was over, they started back home, but the boy Jesus stayed in Jerusalem. His parents did not know this. On the third day they found him in the Temple, sitting with the Jewish teachers, listening to them and asking questions. His parents were astonished when they saw him, and his mother said to him, "Son, why have you done this to us? Your father and I have been terribly worried trying to find you."

Luke 2:41-43, 46, 48

This was a new experience for Mary and Joseph. The challenge was how to relate to this new aspect of Jesus that they had never seen before. Their child was growing and changing, and the ramifications caught them by surprise. They had to let go of what was and learn to accept something new.

Mary experienced change yet again when, many years later, Jesus left home in order to do the work to which his Father called him. As Jesus' ministry developed, Mary saw another aspect of Jesus that she probably had never seen before. She had to adapt herself to a new relation with her son that may have initially caused some bafflement. But it also brought an experience of enrichment as she continued to see new aspects of Jesus' personality unfold. Dealing with change in all its various forms was a part of her life, just as it is a part of ours.

Someone once said that one thing that will never stop changing is change itself. We might prefer stability, especially at a time when things change so fast, but our lives continue to flow like a river whose surging power cannot be stopped. That's a good thing, because change enriches our experience of life by opening us up to ever-new possibilities.

Through all the changes that characterized the relationship between Mary and Jesus, there was one constant: their fidelity to each other. That's the lesson for us, and if we follow it, we come to know the joy of love that allows us to be who we are. Our fidelity to one another takes place in a world of relentless inner and outer change. Love and fidelity are meant to last in the midst of change, but the change colors the way in which our fidelity expresses itself. The fidelity of a married couple at the end of their life journey has a different tone than that of the fidelity they expressed to one another on their wedding day. The same can be said of our fidelity to God as our awareness of him grows. And that is also true of our friendships as the love of our friends evolves. Change can be a positive value in our lives.

Can you see the value of change in your life?

15.

A MATTER OF URGENCY.

He said to another man, "Follow me." But that man said, "Sir, first let me go back and bury my father." Jesus answered, "Let the dead bury their own dead. You go and proclaim the Kingdom of God."

Luke 9:59-60

Imagine that someone you love is in the hospital in critical condition, and you receive a phone call informing you that she may die very soon. You want to see her and speak with her one last time before she dies. At that moment, your priorities change, and there is a sense of urgency that revolves around one goal: getting to that hospital as soon as you can. All other concerns are swallowed up by this overriding need to see the one you love before it is too late.

A similar sense of urgency seems to have influenced the thinking of Jesus concerning his ministry. He may have had an intuition that there would not be much time. His message had to be heard, because people's lives depended on hearing it. And it was his love for all of us that fueled this sense of urgency.

Jesus' message was, and will always be, that God is benevolent, that we are all unconditionally loved, and that God will bring good out of evil. His loving, helping presence will always be with us, helping us to love one another. And his message was crowned with the promise that this life will give way, not to death, but to resurrection and to a fullness of life that will never end. This was the message that had to be heard, and it was so important that a sense of urgency permeated what Jesus said and did.

Our response was a matter of some urgency too. Jesus called us to repent, which meant to rid ourselves of any negative attitudes that would keep us from receiving and living the message. Otherwise, we would lose our ability to love and know joy, and that would mean that we would miss the meaning of our lives.

It is no surprise that Jesus would have felt a sense of urgency in spreading his message. Imagine spending even one day without its consolation. God in his love for us wanted to spare us that kind of pain. When Jesus' sense of urgency to reveal his message is met with our sense of urgency to respond, we have the foundation on which to build a solid, vital spiritual life. Then Jesus' message can bear its fruit in our daily lives. Our lives become meaningful, because God's words within us give birth to love. And it is love that gives a new vitality to the way we think, and to what we say and do.

Is there a sense of urgency in you to hear and to respond more completely to Jesus' message?

16.
KEEP IT SIMPLE.

"Go! I am sending you like lambs among wolves. Don't take a purse or a beggar's bag or shoes; don't stop to greet anyone on the road."

Luke 10:3-4

Jesus tells his disciples to be single-minded about what he asks them to do and not to encumber themselves with unnecessary things. Times change, of course, and what might have been looked upon as unnecessary in Jesus' time might be considered quite necessary in our own. But Jesus' point remains valid, and we can let his words speak to us by asking how we can interpret them in our circumstances today. A fresh sense of freedom and a deeper trust in God would be our reward.

Perhaps in our day, we could see useless worries as part of the baggage that God invites us to throw off. When we believe in God's loving care, we can afford to let them go. The more worries we let go of, the lighter our load becomes, and the more energy we have to do what needs to be done. This makes sense if we ask a few important questions: Does our worry change anything? Would we travel more lightly if we had the faith and courage to let our worries go? How much joy do we lose because we carry the excess baggage of unnecessary fear?

I remember a cartoon that portrayed a nervous man shaking in his seat on a plane, his face contorted with discomfort. Underneath the cartoon was a caption that read, "Note, the plane has not yet left the ground." Compare that with the Zen story of a captured samurai who was scheduled for execution on the day following his capture. He sat calmly in his cell with the thought that his allies might attack his enemies and set him free. But if not, he was determined not to let the calmness of the present moment be destroyed by the thought of what might happen tomorrow. That might seem like super-human mind control, but we do have a certain ability to choose how much mental baggage we are willing to carry.

Keeping life simple by letting go of useless worry doesn't mean that nothing bad will ever happen. It does mean, though, that we can come to realize that many of our worries never come true. And when something bad does happen, we believe that God will always bring good from any evil that will ever touch us. From death, God brings resurrection. From sin, he brings the possibility of repentance. With trust in God, we can travel light, keep our lives simple, and carry within us a sense of peace that becomes inseparable from joy. That's an important part of the gospel's message.

How often do you pray for the grace to keep your life simple?

17.

YOUR LIFE IS MEANT TO REFLECT THE LIGHT OF GOD TO OTHERS.

"You are like light for the whole world."

Mt. 5:14

Jesus calls himself the light of the world, and he tells us that we are like light. Jesus is our light through what he says and does. When we allow his power to work within us, then we become like light for others by what we say and do. That gives us a tremendous dignity. Jesus asks us to reflect his light to others, and the more his love and values shine out to others through us, the more worthwhile our lives become.

We might think that being like light is reserved for those who are healthy, strong, and successful according to the standards of popular culture. But I know a stroke victim who spent seventeen years in an infirmary, and he lived the last two years of his life in pain due to cancer. Visitors to his room were almost always greeted with a welcoming smile. I never heard him complain. He appreciated people who read to him, because that helped him to discover new ideas. His caregivers were deeply affected by the way in which he accepted his illness. They were impressed by his ability to enjoy whatever he could of life, in spite of his illness. This man was like a light to those who knew him. And he was surely like a light to me.

Think about people who are faithful to their families and friends, who honor their commitments even when that becomes difficult, and who serve others at some expense to themselves. They reflect the commitment that God continually shows to us. We know such people, and their example has been a gift for us. We can be grateful that they have been like light in our lives, showing us our possibilities to be like light in the lives of others.

Be grateful for all the ways your life has reflected God's love for others. When you become more aware of how your life has been like a light, you become more grateful for God's goodness to you. For without God's goodness, none of us could ever have given the light to others that God wanted us to give.

Are you aware of the light you have received?

18.

BE OPTIMISTIC ABOUT YOUR LIFE.

"The world will make you suffer. But be brave! I have defeated the world!"

John 16:33

Jesus overcame suffering not by avoiding it, but by going through the suffering he could not avoid. His life demonstrated that suffering is never the last word about our lives, and that God will bring good out of whatever evils we go through. Jesus' suffering and death gave birth to his resurrection. And through his suffering, death, and resurrection, he became the source of our resurrection. The end of our life here is simply the gateway to new life beyond space and time, and so beyond suffering and death.

St. Paul reflected on Jesus' death and resurrection, and then wrote the following powerful lines: "*Where, Death, is your victory? Where, Death, is your power to hurt?*"(I Cor. 15:55.) Johannes Brahms in his magnificent work, *A German Requiem*, has the choir sing these words over and over again in marvelous melodies of faith. We can make these words our own. They bring tremendous joy because they speak of a future that will be full of life, a life free from any pain or death.

An optimistic view of life includes being optimistic not only about ourselves, but also about those whom we love. What is possible for us is also possible for them. God gives all of us the gift of life. We have only to live in harmony with God's will in order to receive the fullness of life he wants to give us. And in that fullness of life, we will always be united with those we love.

We will not be exempt from life's difficulties, but God will work with us to bring the best out of them. We sin, but God gives us the grace of repentance. We make mistakes, but God gives us the guidance

34

to learn from them. We die, but God brings life from death and gives us the new life of the resurrection. And so there is hope, a hope that is the foundation for an optimistic view of life, for Jesus has overcome the world.

Are you optimistic about your life?

19.

PEACE BE WITH YOU.

It was late that Sunday evening, and the disciples were gathered together behind locked doors, because they were afraid of the Jewish authorities. Then Jesus came and stood among them. "Peace be with you," he said.

John 20:19

Peter had denied knowing Jesus. Many of Jesus' disciples were not by the cross when he died. And it seems that all of his disciples had been slow to understand his message. This was not an exceptionally faithful or successful group of people, and yet Jesus appeared to them with a greeting of peace and love. Jesus' appearance was an act of forgiveness. By appearing in their midst, he was showing them that they were still loved and that nothing was being held against them. He was not going to replace them with another group, but they would be given another chance to become what Jesus had called them to be.

Jesus' greeting of peace was a sign of love and forgiveness. It was as if he were saying, "We are still together. Let us continue what we started out to do." But the greeting of peace was also a sign of power. The peace of Jesus empowered the apostles to believe in his forgiveness and to start anew with the joyful task of spreading the kingdom of God.

Peace is Jesus' unchanging greeting to us. He offers it to us always. The greeting tells us that we are forgiven and that through him we have the power to do what he calls us to do. We are always given another chance to set things right. All we have to do is to accept the peace Jesus constantly offers us, and then our guilt is quieted and our hearts are at rest. The ultimate success of our lives is built on the foundation of this acceptance of Jesus' gift of peace. It brings a wonderful sense of relief and joy.

You have probably been blessed with many gifts, but are any of them more important than the gift of Christ's peace?

20.

LET THE POWER OF JESUS SET YOU FREE.

Jesus said to him, "If you want to be perfect, go and sell all you have and give the money to the poor, and you will have riches in heaven; then come and follow me."

Mt. 19:21

Wealth can be a wonderful gift when it is used correctly. The circumstances of each life determine just how that gift should be used. In the case of the rich man in the gospel, Jesus invited him to give all of his wealth to the poor, but the rich man was stuck in his attachment to his wealth, and he was unable to move beyond it. The problem was not about wealth as such, but about attachments to it. What the rich man didn't realize was that he would have gotten more out of life by having less. That is the paradox that dominates his story, and the only way out for him was to let go of what kept him from being free. The story ends tragically, for we are told that the rich man went away sad. The story of the rich man invites us to ask ourselves where we are stuck, and what attachments keep us from being free.

Not all attachments are about wealth. What attachments keep you from being free? Sometimes things that are good in themselves, such as work, pleasure, recreation, or a certain amount of self-interest, can become addictive. We can have too much of these things and become ensnared by them. Paradoxically, we would be better off with less. You can tell when an addiction takes over your life. You lose awareness of other values, like people whose self-interest becomes so encompassing that they fail to notice the needs of others. You also get the feeling that something is missing in your life, and you lose a sense of freedom and joy. When you feel stuck and unable to free yourself from an addiction, what can you do about it?

Jesus acknowledges the difficulty of breaking attachments to wealth, but he gives the answer as to how that can be done. He tells us that what is impossible for man is possible for God. The way out of our powerlessness is to rely on the power of God so that we can be set free from the attachments that bind us. What works in overcoming attachments to wealth also works in overcoming other kinds of attachments. People who belong to Alcoholics Anonymous have this saying: "I can't, God can, I think I'll let him." Of course, counseling and support are crucial in overcoming serious addictions, but reliance on the power of God enables us to increase their fruitfulness.

The gospel often repeats the necessity of relying on God's power. Our success in life depends on our ability to have faith in that power. Our belief in God's power working in our lives is a powerful reason to rejoice, and it is our key to freedom and peace.

Most of us struggle with some kind of an addiction. How do you deal with yours?

21.

BLENDING PRAYER WITH OUR WORK.

"Lord, don't you care that my sister has left me to do all the work by myself? Tell her to come and help me!" The Lord answered her, "Martha, Martha! You are worried and troubled over so many things, but just one is needed. Mary has chosen the right thing, and it will not be taken away from her."

Luke 10:40-42

I can appreciate the dilemma that this story illustrates. At times I have been invited to dinner and found little opportunity to talk with the one who invited me. Kitchen work gobbled up most of the time allotted for the visit. For that reason, sometimes a simple meal might be preferable to an elaborate dinner. Maybe that would have been Jesus' preference. One of Jesus' concerns seemed to be a desire to spend time with Martha, but he found her to be taken up with other concerns. It does seem somewhat of a paradox. All of her busy activity was for him, but at that moment, her busy activity was not what Jesus wanted. He wanted her presence and an opportunity to communicate. And if we look into the heart of God, this is what he wants from all of us. Isn't this the major point of the gospel?

Perhaps Martha could have served Jesus and listened to him at the same time. Jewish houses in Jesus' time were small, and so she could have worked and still had the opportunity to hear and respond. The problem though was that, according to the story, Martha was worried and troubled by many things. The worries would have complicated her ability to be hospitable to Jesus. If she had worked with a quieter mind, would she have been more able to be present to Jesus? If we worked with quieter minds, would we be more aware of God's presence in our lives?

This story shows us that God wants communication with us, and this is a sign of his intimate love. Love always wants to communicate itself. That's why people in love sometimes want to be alone with one another, completely free from outside distractions. We need "alone time" with God too, and Mary recognized that need. But there is also the need to serve, to attend to the requirements of those we love. That's the need Martha recognized. Her challenge, though, was to serve with a quieter mind so that she could have a greater awareness of Jesus' presence as she served. She needed to capture a bit of Mary's attitude. Perhaps that is our challenge too. We can prayerfully ask God to take care of our worries, so that we can let them go. Then we can be present to him and to others without being sidetracked by disquieting distractions. God will certainly respond to this prayer. Actually, the very act of serving others can be a beautiful form of prayer when we offer that service to God with a quiet, loving heart. This is a possible goal to achieve. I know some people who have been quite successful in achieving it. One can bring a prayerful attitude to any kind of work.

Our lives are meant to reflect the attitudes of both Mary and Martha in our relationship with God and with the people we love. How do you achieve this balance in your life?

22.
DOING WHAT GOD DOES.

"I, your Lord and Teacher, have just washed your feet. You, then, should wash one another's feet. I have set an example for you, so that you will do just what I have done for you."

John 13:14-15.

Washing of feet in Jesus' time was a task usually done by servants. But he takes this task into his own hands to make a point. The washing of feet is a symbol of an attitude that is meant to animate our relationships with others. Using our unique talents that we have received, we serve others by sharing our talents with those who need them. Teachers will teach. Healers will heal. Those who have more will share with those who have less. We give and receive from one another, and in that way, we create a community that becomes rich through mutual giving. Imagine how much more beautiful life would be for everyone in our society if we all served in this way. It is crucial for us to know what our gifts are and how others can be enriched through our sharing of what we have received.

By serving others through selfless giving, we do what God does, for in many ways, God is our servant. He serves us by giving us life. He serves us by continuing to preserve us in existence. He serves us through the inspirations of his Holy Spirit. And he serves us through the giving of his word, and through the Sacraments, which are special signs of his presence among us.

It may seem strange to think of God as a servant, but here is an interesting parallel. If you own a dog, you might think of yourself as the dog's master. Yet, if you want the dog to thrive, you will feed him regularly, let him out when he needs that, take him to the vet to keep him well, and play with him to keep him from becoming bored. If you do all of those things, you might well ask, who is serving whom?

We are called to serve just as the Master Server serves us. Did you ever think of God as one who serves you? Considering the gifts you have and the needs of others around you, how can you best imitate God in your daily life?

23.

YOUR LIFE IS WHAT YOU MAKE IT TO BE.

"A good person out of the store of goodness in his heart produces good, but an evil person out of a store of evil produces evil."

Luke 6:45

What an opportunity is yours! After God brings you into life, he gives you the power to work with him in the task of forming yourself. Together with God, you build yourself into a person whose heart produces goodness. It is a grand partnership. All of your choices are important, for they determine the level of goodness that will form your life, as well as the level of happiness you will be able to enjoy.

The most important choices we make are those concerned with relationships: our relationships with God, with other people, with ourselves, and with our environment. If we look at our lives from this perspective, we find meaning in the harmony we choose to have with God and with others. The alternative is to choose to live for ourselves without regard for anyone or anything that lies beyond our private concerns. It is a choice that never brings lasting happiness, because the scope of the choice is too small. We are made for a much greater experience of life. Our life journey becomes successful when we stretch beyond ourselves, doing for the happiness of others what we would do for our own. Living in this way, we build our lives on the word of God, and we join the ranks of those whose hearts produce goodness. Nothing can shake a heart like that, for its foundation is built on God's word.

From time to time, it helps to reflect about the direction in which our life journeys are going, and what it is that our hearts are producing. The direction may be positive and life-giving, but it could also be negative because sometimes we lose sight of what is meaningful to us. We don't always realize when we are on the wrong track, even though there are early warning signs. Dissatisfaction with our lives can be one of those signs. It would seem impossible for people to be satisfied with their lives when they are not in harmony with God, or with the persons and things around them. But the dissatisfaction has a value. It alerts us to the possibility that we may not be making choices that are really in our best interest. And the good news is that we can change if we really want to do so.

Do your choices bring you a sense of peace and fulfillment?

24.

YOU HAVE BEEN CHOSEN FOR MEMBERSHIP IN HEAVEN.

"There are many rooms in my Father's house, and I am going to prepare a place for you."

John 14:2

Your being chosen for membership in heaven is a cause for great joy in this present moment, but it has its roots in the distant past. The choice for your membership was made by God long before you were born. From the beginning of time your Creator knew and loved you. And when you were born, his plan for you took flesh and became visible. The plan was that your relationship with him should be without end. Not even your death could disrupt God's purpose, for in his mind, death was simply to be a gateway that leads to fuller life.

Consistency in loving is the ultimate mark of God's love, and Jesus revealed the meaning that this consistency has for us. He told us that there were many mansions in his Father's house, and that he was going to prepare a place for us so that our lives would always be entwined with his. He intended our relationship with him to be permanent, for once we arrived at our mansion, nothing would ever be able to pull us away.

Our nomination for membership in heaven is a marvelous sign of how deeply God cherishes us. If God loves us all with such consistency, then we have a clear sign of our value in God's eyes. Is there any reason, then, why we should not value both one another and ourselves? God loves us even with our sins and faults, but if we choose to remain caught in their traps, we will not be free to return God's love. Here is the great tragedy about life. We can be surrounded by love and yet refuse to be influenced by it. The ultimate tragedy is that we can even refuse our nomination for membership in heaven.

No matter what we decide, we have no power to stop God from loving us. But we do have the tremendous power to accept or reject God's love. Our being chosen for membership in heaven is the most beautiful gift that will ever be given to us, and our decision to accept it is the most important decision we will ever make.

A room in God's mansion is ready for you if you want it. How deeply do you appreciate this promise of unending joy with God, and with all those you love?

25.

YOUR EXPECTATIONS DETERMINE HOW YOU EXPERIENCE GOD'S PRESENCE IN YOUR LIFE.

At that time there was a man named Simeon living in Jerusalem. He was a good, God-fearing man and was waiting for Israel to be saved. The Holy Spirit was with him and had assured him that he would not die before he had seen the Lord's promised Messiah.

Luke 2:25-26

This is a beautiful story about expectation. Simeon hears the promise that he will see the Messiah, and at that point, his life is taken over by this expectation. At the end of Simeon's life, Mary and Joseph bring the child Jesus into the Temple, and Simeon immediately recognizes him as the one for whom he had been waiting. If his expectation had not sharpened his spiritual and physical senses, would he have been able to recognize Jesus so quickly?

Our expectations influence our experiences of life. Would a person marry if he had no expectations that the marriage would bring him and his wife a measure of mutual fulfillment and happiness? Who would prepare for a career if she had no expectations that her preparations would be successful and bring a sense of accomplishment? This also holds true in our relationships with God. Without our expectation and desire, no relationship can take root.

But one caveat needs to be considered. Expectations that center primarily on our ego fulfillment will sell us short. If someone were to enter marriage with primary expectation of his own fulfillment, without thought of his partner's happiness, his expectation would bear bitter fruit. I think it is the same in our relationship with God. If our expectation were to center only on our own fulfillment and not on

God's glory and the fidelity we owe to him, we would simply get more bitter fruit. Too much self-seeking ruins our ability to find joy in any relationship, because then we are left just with ourselves. Not much joy in that! It seems that we can only find genuine joy when we are more concerned about bringing joy to others rather than to ourselves.

Perhaps this is a good time to ask yourself about your expectations. Where do you put your energies? What are your hopes and your dreams? It is true, of course, that not all of our hopes and dreams can be realized in this life. We need to choose them wisely. Simeon discovered his dream when he received it from God. It was God who told him that he would not die before he would see the Messiah.

Most likely we will not receive such direct revelations in our own lives, but a prayerful openness to God will prepare us to intuit his guidance in the midst of our dilemmas. And we have received the words of Jesus promising us that he would be with us in the present and lead us into the future. And so, the big question is: Do your expectations open your heart to believe that God will fulfill his promises to you?

26.

SUCCESS IN LIFE COMES FROM A PARTNERSHIP WITH GOD.

"Ask, and you will receive; seek, and you will find; knock, and the door will be opened to you."

Mt. 7:7

A boy decided to build a small table as a birthday gift for his mother. Since this was the boy's first attempt at carpentry, his father offered to help him. But he refused, saying that he knew what to do from watching his father at work, and that he was capable of making the table on his own. The boy worked hard, but his unaided skills were not up to the task. When he finished, the table legs were uneven and the table wobbled. The boy's gift did not turn out as he had planned.

The mature person recognizes his limitations, realizing that sometimes he needs to ask for help. As a person matures and grows in faith, he understands that the success of his accomplishments is rooted in the strength God gives him, and he asks for that strength in all that he does. Peace and a measure of success are the fruits of his reaching out for help. If you see such a person, you are likely to respect him for who he is and what he does. His life's success is the result of a partnership with God, without whom no success would be possible.

We can make a conscious decision to live our lives in a partnership with God, who works in us to accomplish what is good. This is one of the most important decisions that we ever have to make, and it will have a decisive effect on our daily lives. Our failures are often the result of our decision to live life by our own strength alone. We sometimes forget that our success comes from God, who wants to work with us in all that we do.

Do you try at times to live your life like the boy who tried to build a table on his own?

27.

JESUS CALLS YOU TO FOLLOW HIM, JUST AS YOU ARE.

Jesus left that place, and as he walked long, he saw a tax collector, named Matthew, sitting in his office. He said to him, "Follow me." Matthew got up and followed him.

Mt. 9:9

In Jesus' society, tax collectors were not regarded with respect. They gathered money from the Jews and gave it to the Roman occupiers who controlled their country. Some of them gathered more than what was required by the Romans, and then lined their own pockets with the surplus. No wonder that tax collectors were near the bottom rung of the social ladder. It was one of these tax collectors, a man named Matthew, whom Jesus called to follow him.

We can be thankful that Jesus included Matthew among his apostles, because this shows that Jesus doesn't mind having imperfect people among those he chooses to follow him. In fact, he actually seeks them out. The good news for us is that, with all our imperfections, we too are called to follow him. We too fit into Jesus' plan, just as we are at this present moment. Such is the power of God's love.

The good news does not stop with this. When Jesus called Matthew, he gave him the ability to grow out of his imperfections into the person that Jesus wanted him to become. Matthew said "yes" to this part of the call too. The same is true for us. Every day we are flooded with the power of God, which enables us to grow into the persons Jesus wants us to become. That power is never lacking to us. We have only to say yes to it.

It is difficult to comprehend the immense beauty of this divine love that accepts you just as you are, and then helps you to grow beyond yourself. What a cause for joy! How often do you thank God for showering you with such a life-giving love?

28.

EVEN TROUBLES CAN BE BLESSINGS.

"Do not think that I have come to bring peace to the world. No, I did not come to bring peace, but a sword."

Mt. 10:34

Here you have one of the great paradoxes of the gospel. The main message of Jesus throughout the gospel is one of peace. But Jesus' statement about bringing a sword seems like a contradiction of that message. The sword, however, would seem to be inseparable from the gospel, because the gospel will at times be a stumbling block, both to ourselves and to others. People will be divided among themselves by differing interpretations of Jesus' words, or even by different religions. Individuals will be divided within themselves because various pockets of self-centeredness will make it hard for them to choose what is good. I have experienced these divisions within myself, and I would be surprised if you had not at times experienced them too.

Religious differences have divided families and communities throughout history. We can imagine the damage that these have caused. But suppose people confronted their differences not with enmity but with understanding. For example, my study of Eastern religions has resulted in a deeper appreciation of Christianity. I have been enriched by the insights I have gained from Eastern religions, and they have helped me in my spiritual journey as a Christian. And even some of the irreconcilable differences have led me to a deeper appreciation of what I hold to be true. Religious divisions and differences can sometimes cause trouble, or they can result in a deeper appreciation of the gift of faith that is our truth.

Perhaps some of the most painful divisions exist deep within the individual himself. One can be divided within himself when his thoughts and actions are at odds with the words of Jesus. That division can cut like a sword. But the sword's pain can be a blessing if one learns from it. The pain coming from a bad or misinformed conscience can lead to a conversion, which gives rise to peace of mind and heart. And the pain that comes from the embarrassing experience of weakness can lead to a deeper desire for God's saving help.

Jesus does say that the sword, or troubles, will be a part of our lives. But he does not say that they will be the final word about our lives. In this life, he promises to be with us always, and we rely on the divine help that this implies. In the next life, troubles will have no place. In the meantime, we can learn from them, and in that sense, they can sometimes be a blessing.

Difficulties will always be a part of your life. Would it make sense to try to learn something from them?

29.
WE ARE RELATIVES OF JESUS.

Jesus answered, "Who is my mother? Who are my brothers?" Then he pointed to his disciples and said, "Look! Here are my mother and my brothers! Whoever does what my Father in heaven wants him to do is my brother, my sister, and my mother."

Mt. 12:48-50

One could ask what it is that most truly makes one a member of a family. It might seem that being born into a family would be the crucial point. But suppose that there were two sons, one who belongs to the family by birth, and the other who is adopted into it. Suppose further that the former repudiates all that his family stands for, while the latter accepts all its values and enters fully into the family's life. Which of the two would be more a member of that family?

Jesus defines who the members of his family are, and this is good news indeed. It says a lot about what God calls us to be. What unites us to Jesus is our sharing in his values, and this is what makes us members of his family. To belong is a matter of choice, and this is the choice Jesus invites us to make. In making that choice, we clearly define who we are, and the dignity that comes from that choice is truly breathtaking.

If we are related to Jesus through our doing of the Father's will, then we are related to all those who embrace the values of Jesus. We are members of an illustrious family of countless individuals who share in our choice. This too gives us a deeper idea of who we are, and how profoundly we are related to others.

Have you ever thought of yourself as one of Jesus' relatives?

30.

KNOWING WHERE TO FIND REST.

"Come to me, all of you who are tired of carrying heavy loads, and I will give you rest."

Mt. 11:28

Is there anyone who hasn't asked for relief when the load of life just seems to be too heavy? The answer does not always result in the removal of the load. I think quite often the answer comes through the help God gives in changing our attitudes about the load.

A Zen master once admitted that for many years he had been burdened occasionally with feelings of anger. But after years of Zen practice, the burden was lightened. "So now you no longer feel angry?" one of his students asked. "Oh no," the master replied. "The anger still comes back at times. But I don't let it bother me anymore."

Perhaps we have a personality defect like anger or laziness that we do our best to overcome, but some part of it remains with us, no matter what we do. Would it be possible for us to pray for the gift to accept ourselves as we are, while still gently trying to move beyond our defect? Living with this kind of an attitude, we would find the rest that we crave.

Perhaps we watch a loved one making choices that will cause her pain, but nothing we say or do motivates her to change. While praying that she might finally make healthier choices, could we also pray to let go of what, at the moment, we cannot change? We could place our loved one in God's hands, for he loves her more than we do. And we could pray for the strength to let go of some of our load of sorrow and disappointment. Carrying that load benefits no one, but when we love someone deeply, it can be very hard to let it go. That's why we come to the one who tells us that he can help us to let go. And that is one of the ways in which he gives us rest.

We live in a world that is often restless, and we add to the restlessness by carrying loads we need not carry. Jesus invites us to come to him for relief and the ability to let go. Wouldn't it make sense to take him up on his invitation?

31.

THE VALUE OF AN OPEN HEART.

At that time Jesus said, "Father, Lord of heaven and earth! I thank you because you have shown to the unlearned what you have hidden from the wise and learned!"

Mt. 11-25

A Samurai warrior came to a Zen master and asked to be instructed in the wisdom of Zen. The Zen master smiled, invited his visitor to sit down, and then began to pour tea into a small cup. The cup was nearly full, and the master continued to pour. The tea ran over into the saucer, but the master continued to pour. Finally the tea began to spill onto the table, and still the master continued to pour. "Stop!" the warrior commanded. "Can't you see the cup is full? You can't get more in unless you empty it!" "And how can I teach you the truth about life," the master answered, "unless you first become empty of yourself?"

Perhaps the master saw that the warrior was merely curious, that he was too full of his own ideas about life to make room for something new. In that sense, the warrior needed to become empty. There would be no other way for him to have an open heart able to receive what the master had to say.

The situation in Jesus' time offers a parallel to the Zen story. Many of the learned at that time seemed not to be open to his message. In contrast, the unlearned seemed to be the ones who were open and receptive. They were sufficiently empty to make room in their hearts for something new, and that enabled them to benefit from what they heard. All that was required was an attitude of openness.

The good news is that one doesn't have to be learned or even successful in order to receive the joy of Jesus' message. He offers his message and his presence to all who come to him with an open heart, much in the same way as the sun shines into every eye that is open to receive its rays. Those who hear with an open heart are the ones whose lives are beautifully affected by the light of what Jesus says. They gain not only information, but also a new way of thinking, feeling, and acting that changes their lives in a wonderful way. This is the experience that Jesus offers to each one of us. We have only to accept it.

An open heart is one that is empty enough to receive and to be affected by what is said. How open is your heart to the words God addresses to you?

32.

SOMETIMES THIRTY PERCENT IS ENOUGH.

"And the seeds sown in the good soil stand for those who hear the message and understand it: They bear fruit, some as much as one hundred, others sixty, and others thirty."

Mt. 13:23

I have always found this to be a consoling part of Jesus' message, because in some areas of my life, I have been a thirty "percenter." Sometimes I look at what the hundred "percenters" have accomplished, and then compare that to what I have done. I have been told that this isn't the proper thing to do to oneself, but to some extent, it works. Looking at the accomplishments of others has prodded me to do better in some areas of my life than I otherwise might have done. If that helped me to reach thirty **percent**, and if thirty **percent** was the result of my best efforts, then I have used my talents well.

A confrere of mine illustrated this idea with the following example: Suppose that a family has two children in school. One child is intellectually gifted and gets straight A's on his report card. He is rewarded with praise and sometimes even with a gift. The other child is a mediocre student who gets only C's. But he works hard, doing the best with the ability he has. However, he receives no reward at all. My confrere asked, "Shouldn't this child also receive some acknowledgment for his achievement? After all, he worked hard consistently and did the best with what he had."

My confrere had a valid point. Perhaps this could change the harsh way in which we sometimes evaluate ourselves. If we have done the best with what we have, we should honor the results of our efforts, even if the results are thirty percent. As Jesus tells the parable about the good seed that bears fruit, he never condemns the seed that bears only thirty percent. The good seed bears fruit according to its ability. We do the same. It seems that God is pleased with us if we do the best we can, not matter how the percentages turn out. Perhaps this is another way of saying that God accepts our best efforts, even when they do not produce as much fruit as we might like. Maybe we could do the same for ourselves, giving thanks for whatever we have been able to accomplish. Maybe we could even do that in our evaluation of others, letting them know that we appreciate whatever their best efforts were able to achieve.

God never demands more of you than you can do. If God is content with the results of your best efforts, can you be content with them too?

33.

YOU HAVE ALL THE SIGNS YOU NEED.

Some Pharisees came to Jesus and started to argue with him. They wanted to trap him, so they asked him to perform a miracle to show that God approved of him. But Jesus gave a deep groan and said, "Why do the people of this day ask for a miracle? No, I tell you. No such proof will be given to these people."

Mark 8:11-12

What can you give to somebody who already has so much? The Pharisees had already seen the splendid results of Jesus' ministry, but they wanted yet another sign. Perhaps Jesus thought they had been shown enough, especially since they seemed not to appreciate what they had. I can think of at least one modern parallel that perhaps many of us have experienced in our lives. Imagine a child with a room full of toys who complains that he has nothing to do. His solution is to ask for another toy. Just like the Pharisees! Perhaps just like us! The proper solution would be not to add something new, but rather to appreciate what is already in front of us.

Sometimes in the midst of boredom or distress, we ask for a special sign of God's loving presence in our lives. But do we really need more than we already have? As I look out of my window, I see a beautiful blue sky brushed by treetops gently swaying in the wind. As I look downward, I can see the bushes and colorful flowers that are always a part of summer's gift. The point, though, is that all of these things are gifts from a loving God, but they would be somewhat useless to me if I were not aware of them.

Today I also celebrated the Eucharist with people who deeply appreciate receiving the Sacrament of Christ's body and blood. And this is a gift present in my life every day. This evening I am having dinner with people whose friendship has deeply enriched my life. Friendships are yet another example of God's gifts that are reflections of his love for us. God has shown his goodness in still other ways today, and it's only 3:30 p.m.!

I have shared these experiences as an invitation for you to look at your own day. How have you experienced God's goodness today? If you are thankfully aware of God's blessings, perhaps you can say God has done more than enough. We need no further signs from him as a proof of his love. But we do need a deep awareness of what has already been given.

Are you aware of the signs of God's love that you already have, or are you looking for more?

34.

USE WISELY WHAT HAS BEEN GIVEN TO YOU.

*"Then the servant who had received one thousand coins
came in and said, 'Sir, I know you are a hard man; you
reap harvests where you did not plant, and you gather
crops where you did not scatter seed. I was afraid, so I
went off and hid your money in the ground. Look! Here
is what belongs to you.' 'You bad and lazy servant!' his
master said. 'You should have deposited my money in the
bank, and I would have received it all back with interest
when I returned.'"*

Mt. 25:24-27

In this parable of the three servants, all three received a sum of
coins that was meant to be increased for the master's benefit. The
first two servants invested well, and their efforts paid off. The master
benefited from their efforts, and the servants were rewarded for their
good work. The third servant was lazy, and he missed his opportunity
to do something meaningful with what he had been given. The results
of his missed opportunity are recorded in the scriptural quote given
above.

The good news is that each one of us has been given gifts that we
are to use for God's glory, and for the good of others. I think that is
part of the message of Jesus' parable. Some have the gift to be teachers.
Others are given the gift to heal, either through the use of medical
means or through prayer. Others are given the gift of expertise in
business and commerce. If those gifts are used for the common good,
they are important for the building of community. There are, of course,
many other gifts we have been given that are to be used for the welfare
of others. And just as the servants in the parable benefit from the use

of their gifts through the reward they receive, so we benefit in a similar way. Our reward is in the knowledge that our lives are meaningful, and in the respect we receive from living a life meaningful for others. God gives the gifts, and we experience the reward from using them wisely.

The third servant lets his gifts lie dormant, and so he misses his reward. This too is a part of the parable's message. Maybe we could ask ourselves if there is a bit of the third servant in us. Suppose we have the gift to help someone who needs us, and we don't use the gift. It could be too that we haven't taken time to develop our special talents that could have been used for the good of others. Some soul-searching could be helpful here, because there is still time to take new directions if that would be needed.

Do you make adequate use of the talents God has given you? If not, do you realize that there is still time to change?

35.

How to become great.

So Jesus called them all together to him and said, "You know that the men who are considered rulers of the heathen have power over them, and the leaders have complete authority. This, however, is not the way it is among you. If one of you wants to be great, he must be the servant of the rest."

Mark 10:42-43

The desire to dominate and control others seems to be well-embedded in human nature. You see this at work in families, in political and social organizations, and perhaps at times even in the Church. Understandably, though, this desire to dominate does create problems and great unrest for those who are dominated. But what is less understood, is that it also creates problems for those who dominate. In fact, any behavior that fattens up the ego never gets the satisfaction it tries to achieve. The miser never gets enough wealth. The pleasure seeker never gets enough pleasure. The power seeker never gets enough power. The dominator never gets enough control. And all of them are often afraid of losing what they have. It seems that the best way to fail in life is to spend it in seeking yourself. Jesus wanted to spare his disciples from that. And so he told them to forget themselves and to direct their energies toward serving the needs of others.

One who serves brings happiness to those he serves. But he also brings happiness to himself. It seems that the accumulated wisdom of the human race bears this out. But it is important that we experience this wisdom not just theoretically in our heads, but more especially in the way in which we live our daily lives. For those who are mature, giving is more pleasurable and satisfying than getting. You can test this out by reflecting on your own life. Compare the times when you lived selfishly with the times when you lived with concern for others. Which attitude brought you more happiness and contentment?

Those who serve others are called "great" because they do more for society than those who live merely for themselves. The great ones are the happy ones, because they do **good** for others, and that brings them joy. Families and societies suffer when there is a lack of great ones, a lack of those who serve. We are all enriched by those who expend their energies for others. And in doing good for others, they reflect the goodness of God to those they serve.

Does Jesus' idea of greatness seem at odds with the ideas of our contemporary society? How would your own life measure up to Jesus' standard of greatness?

36.

BY CARRYING THE CROSS, YOU WILL FIND YOUR JOY.

Then Jesus called the crowd and the disciples to him. "If anyone wants to come with me," he told them, "he must forget himself, carry his cross, and follow me."

Mark 8:34

Carrying the cross may not seem like a good way to experience joy. But we often have to embrace some aspects of the cross in order to achieve things that are important to us. A student may spend many uncomfortable nights, month after month, preparing himself for a degree that is necessary for his career. A follower of Jesus may need to painfully root out some addiction so that he can follow Jesus with greater freedom and with an open heart. In these examples, the difficulties endured are like the carrying of the cross. One carries it because that's the way to reach a desired goal that brings a sense of joy.

Sometimes we carry the cross not to attain something good for ourselves, but rather to respond to the needs of others. A mother may sit up with a sick child night after night, taking care of him so that he can get well and enjoy his life. She does this out of love, but still she does it at some cost to herself. At times, we can only serve others at some cost to ourselves, and that is an aspect of carrying the cross. The benefits come not only to those for whom it is carried, but also to the one who carries it.

I find it important to look at the cross in this way, because when I was younger, Jesus' insistence that we carry the cross seemed negative and disturbing to me. When I look at his words now, they seem not only to be necessary, but also life-giving. In all of the examples above, the carrying of the cross would ultimately result in joy for those who carried it willingly. The cross is not a joy in itself, but it leads to a result that will be joyful. It is the result that makes the carrying of the cross meaningful.

We can try to avoid necessary crosses, but then we simply create greater ones. If we fail to root out the selfishness that interferes with following Christ, then we would have to carry a much heavier cross of regret and loss of peace. Jesus wanted to spare us this kind of pain. That's why he gave us his life-giving words about the cross. Carrying it can be a pathway that ultimately leads to joy.

It can be hard to accept the necessity for the cross in your life. Are you willing to ask for God's help when you experience the temptation to avoid your particular cross?

37.

LIFE GOES BETTER WITH PRAYER.

After sending the people away, he went up a hill by himself to pray. When evening came, Jesus was there alone.

Mt. 14:23

A sense of urgency marked Jesus' ministry. People desperately needed to hear God's word, and Jesus had so little time to give it to them. And yet, he took time to pray. Jesus' human nature needed to be nourished through intimate contact with his Father. He needed to balance activity with silence, and he needed to experience his Father's presence not only through his work, but also through quiet prayer.

Jesus' fidelity to prayer in his life illustrates the importance of prayer in our lives. We need to find God's presence not only in the people and things around us, but also within ourselves as Jesus did. I think we never become fully conscious of God's presence if we fail to look for him in both ways. It is easy to rationalize that we have no time to do this. We tell ourselves that we have too many responsibilities, and that our activities are necessary for the good of others. These are interesting arguments, but they did not sway Jesus. His work was certainly not less important than ours, and yet he took time to pray.

Jesus did his Father's work as he spread his message, but his human nature needed his Father's power in order to bring that work to completion. We try to complete the work that God has given us to do, and we too need the Father's power in order to be successful. That power comes to us through prayer. This message runs through the entire gospel, and Jesus taught it both by his words and by his example.

There are different ways to pray, and we have to find the ways that best fit our personalities and our life situations. Some prefer silence while others prefer to use words. Many books have been written about the various kinds of prayer, and it would be helpful to be familiar with them. A spiritual director can be of great help in guiding us through the difficulties that come up as we try to find the best way to deepen our life of prayer. Sometimes prayer becomes difficult because we try to pray in a way that isn't harmonious with our personalities or compatible with our level of spiritual development. And so we may need to experiment for a time until we find a form of prayer that is in harmony with who we are. It is worth the effort, because prayer helps us to experience God's presence in a more intimate way and gives us the strength to do what God want us to do.

Do you appreciate the value of prayer in your life?

38.
GIVE YOUR FEARS TO GOD.

The disciples had rowed about three or four miles when they saw Jesus walking on the water, coming near the boat, and they were terrified. "Don't be afraid," Jesus told them, "it is I!"

John 6:19-20

Life contains many experiences that bring us joy and delight, but it also harbors experiences that cause fear. There's the fear of saying the wrong thing to someone you love. Then there is the fear of failure that haunts some of us, and for others it may be the fear of losing one's youth and growing old. And who hasn't been touched by the fear of sickness or death? None of us is immune from some kind of fear that saps our energies and clouds our joys. That's why Jesus tells us often, "Don't be afraid." Easier said than done, of course. How, then, can we follow these words of Jesus and find more of his peace in our lives?

Years ago I visited a woman who was dying of cancer. I was enrolled in a course of clinical pastoral education at the time, and the director told us that when visiting a dying person, we should gently try to see if there were any unresolved issues of fear. After a few minutes I asked her, rather clumsily, if she had any fears that she might want to talk about. I will never forget the peaceful look on her face as she replied, "No. I'm not afraid. I'm ready to go." I didn't know this woman well, and so I don't know what the inner process was that brought her to this peaceful state. I can suppose, though, that she had found a way to give her fears to God, and to trust that her death would lead to a resurrected life. I can still see the look of peace that made her elderly face beautiful. She had learned how to take Jesus' words and make them an integral part of her life.

We can't avoid all feelings of fear, but we can avoid allowing fear to drain our energies. We can refuse to let fear keep us from doing what needs to be done. The Scriptures tell us that Jesus felt great fear in the garden of Gethsemane on the night before he died. But he was able to live through his fear and accomplish our redemption. This was the work of the Father working through his Son Jesus. The Father's power works through us too. We need only to believe that God brings good out of evil, life out of death, and trust out of fear. No need to be afraid, then, if Jesus is with us.

Do you call on Jesus to help you through your fears?

39.

JESUS CONSIDERS YOU TO BE A GIFT FROM HIS FATHER!

"Father! You have given them to me, and I want them to be with me where I am, so that they may see my glory, the glory you gave me; for you loved me before the world was made."

John 17:24

The Father gave us to Jesus, and so we are the Father's gifts to Jesus. These words sound incredible, and it may be hard for us to imagine that this is who we are. But these are Jesus' words, and so when we look into the open heart of God, this is what we see. Understanding and accepting ourselves as gifts show us yet another path that leads us to joy.

When you have a great love for someone, you see that person as a gift in your life. The gift may have blemishes and imperfections, but that doesn't matter so much when you love. If we see our loved ones in this way, it should not be so difficult for us to understand how Jesus sees us.

There is no time limit on this love, for Jesus wants his gifts from the Father to be with him always. Jesus wants us with him beyond this life into the life of the resurrection, where our relationships will never be touched by death. When we love another deeply, we want that relationship to endure. That is what Jesus wants for us.

The tremendous beauty of Jesus' words will probably always be somewhat beyond our full grasp, for we will never be able to understand love in quite the same way as God does. But our understanding can grow if we are willing to meditate on his words. When our minds are focused, quiet, and prayerful, we are better able to experience the movement of God's Spirit in our minds and hearts. The Spirit enables us to understand the meaning of Jesus' words. He waits for us to listen.

Have you ever seriously thought of yourself as the Father's gift to Jesus?

40.

FINDING WHAT IS IMPORTANT.

"Do not store up riches for yourselves here on earth, where moths and rust destroy, and robbers break in and steal. Instead, store up riches for yourselves in heaven, where moths and rust cannot destroy, and robbers cannot break in and steal. For your heart will always be where your riches are."

Mt. 6:19-21

In 1949, General Motors produced one of the most beautifully designed cars of the day. It was a Pontiac hardtop coupe with a wrap-around rear window, a design feature unique for its time. A friend of mine was so enthralled with this car that he said he would be willing to do almost anything to own one. Some years later, the image of this car and the memory of his enthusiasm came back to me. I envisioned where those cars are now, and what they might look like if they were still around. Most of them have completely disappeared, having been recycled one or more times after turning into rusted pieces of junk. Jesus was right. Rust does destroy. What a waste of energy if we give too much enthusiasm for something that will eventually turn ugly and let us down.

This is not to deny that manufactured things are beautiful and can bring temporary joys. But sometimes we expect more of them than they can give. The initial emotional rush they bring slowly fades away, and we become tired of them. And even in the rare cases when this may not be completely true, we can't take them with us when we die. So what is it that we can take with us? What is it that moths and rust cannot destroy? What is it that lasts?

The genuine love that we have given to others, and that others have given to us: this is what we can take with us when we die. This is what lasts. The love that I have received from God, and from my parents and friends, has formed me to be who I am. That will always last, and that is what I will take with me when I die. The same is true for whatever love I have been able to give to others. That will be a part of them forever. No rust can ever destroy that.

I think this is what Jesus had in mind when he said that we should store up riches for ourselves in heaven. We can see how important this is when we consider how we have been touched and formed by the love of others. Nothing is more life-giving than the mutual giving and receiving of love. It is the supreme pathway to the meaning and joy that we are meant to have. If this truth becomes an essential part of who we are, it will determine the way in which we live.

Ask yourself what is most important to you in your life. Do Jesus' words give you a deeper sense of your life's meaning?

41.

APPRECIATING WORDLESS REVELATIONS.

Six days later Jesus took with him Peter and the brothers James and John and led them up a high mountain where they were alone. As they looked on, a change came over Jesus: His face was shining like the sun, and his clothes were dazzling white.

Mt. 17:1-2

Jesus made this beautiful revelation of his inner self without uttering a word. The light streaming from the body of Jesus spoke more deeply to the apostles than any collection of words could have done. Wordless revelations can tell us much about the inner life of a person, and if we are awake, we can find many examples in our lives that illustrate this phenomenon.

A friend of mine went to pick up a pair of glasses she had taken into a store for repair. When she asked for the bill, she was told that there was no charge. After she thanked the salesperson and asked why, the salesperson said, "It's because of your face. Your face shows that you seem to have it all together and that you're enjoying your life. You're an inspiration to me. So I want to do this for you. There's no charge."

What the salesperson said about my friend was true. Her face did reflect what was inside of her. While expending a lot of energy caring for two invalids in her home, she maintained a delightful sense of humor, and she did enjoy her life. Her sense of balance and commitment reflected beautifully on her face. And the salesperson was deeply affected by what she noticed.

Jesus allowed his three disciples to see the revelation of his inner beauty shining outwardly on his face. Jesus' transfiguration was his gift to them, because it revealed at greater depth the beauty of who he was. We too reveal outwardly the inner beauty that lies deep within ourselves. That reflection of our inner life is our gift to others, because it not only reveals who we are; it also reveals to others what they might become.

What kind of a reflection do you suppose people see when they look at you?

42.

WE ARE TRULY ALIVE ONLY WHEN WE GROW.

Jesus told them another parable: "The Kingdom of heaven is like this. A man takes a mustard seed and sows it in his field. It is the smallest of all seeds, but when it grows up, it is the biggest of all plants."

Mt. 13:31-32

Where there is vitality, there you find growth. The first group of Jesus' followers was quite small, but their vitality, nourished by the Holy Spirit, attracted so many that the Kingdom spread throughout the world. Growth is God's plan for the Kingdom, and growth is God's plan for each of the Kingdom's members.

Our faith starts out small like the mustard seed, but what a tragedy if that is the way it remains. Our bodies grow, our understanding of the world grows, but sometimes our knowledge of God remains like it was when we were children. The power of God is within us, nourishing our potential for spiritual growth, but this doesn't happen without our cooperation.

Much of my own understanding of God has grown through reflecting on how God has worked in my life. There is an old saying that goes like this: When the disciple is ready, the teacher will appear. I think that God often works in our lives by bringing us wise people and insightful books whose guidance helps us to grow. For me, the books sometimes came as unexpected gifts, but at other times I've gone to bookstores and libraries, and said a prayer that God would guide me to what I needed to read. I owe much to those who have shared their wisdom with me, either orally or through the written word.

For those who prefer fewer words rather than more, booklets with brief, daily readings are a great help for growth in faith. *Living Faith* is a good example. But no matter what you read, take time for prayerful reflection on what you've read. Then the ideas grow in you and become a part of your life.

Is the seed of faith growing in you, or is it lying dormant?

43.

WE GET MORE THAN WE DESERVE.

"These men who were hired last worked only one hour,"
they said, "while we put up with a full day's work in the
hot sun—yet you paid them the same as you paid us!"

Mt. 20:13

You can get the main point of this parable by reflecting on the good fortune of those who received a full day's pay for only one hour's work. They certainly got more than they deserved. But then, so do we. That is the way God acts toward all of us, giving us a multitude of blessings that goes beyond our expectations.

This idea is beautifully expressed in Seder celebrations. Here are some examples:

If only the Lord God had taken us from Egypt and not executed judgment on the Egyptians,

It would have been enough!

If only the Lord God had executed judgment on the Egyptians and not divided the sea for us,

It would have been enough!

If only the Lord God had divided the sea for us and not watched over us and fed us manna in the desert for forty years,

It would have been enough!

If only the Lord God had watched over us and fed us manna in the desert for forty years and not given us the Sabbath rest,

It would have been enough!

If only the Lord God had given us the Sabbath rest and not given us the Torah,

It would have been enough!

If only the Lord God had given us the Torah and not brought us into the land of Israel,

It would have been enough!
For each and all of these, we say,
It would have been enough!

Perhaps you could rewrite the above prayer and substitute a description of the blessings that God gave to you. You could take any one of your blessings and say, "It would have been enough." But in God's eyes, it wasn't enough. He added so much more. If we look at our blessings in this way, we see how we get more than we deserve, and we see how deeply we are loved. Awareness of our blessings is a beautiful pathway to joy.

Are you aware that you get more than you deserve?

44.

TAKE ADVANTAGE OF YOUR OPPORTUNITIES WHILE YOU CAN.

"As long as it is day, we must do the work of him who sent me; night is coming when no one can work."

John 9:4

It was after midnight and I was having a pleasant walk on our Holy Cross Village property, until I noticed a tall security guard eyeing me with suspicion. I thought it might be prudent to introduce myself to him, and I found out that this was his first night on duty. When he saw that I posed no threat, he told me about his life. He was twenty-six years old, had been in the army, and was consumed now with a strong desire to lead a deeper spiritual life. For six months he had watched no television, and he had read several dozen books that dealt with spirituality. I was amazed at his disciplined determination and at his ability to focus on what was so important to him. There was a sense of urgency in his spiritual quest, a sense that the present moment offered him an opportunity for learning that might not come again. And I learned from him, because it seemed to me that he was putting more emphasis on his spiritual growth than I was putting on mine. He was using his time well.

Jesus reminds us that night is coming when no one can work. The implication is that we need to take advantage of the opportunities life presents to us in this moment and to avoid procrastination, or else we may not be able to accomplish what we would like to do. God gave abilities and potentials to each of us. To live life well would mean to develop those potentials, both for the sake of others, as well as for ourselves. Here is a course of action that would afford a sense of meaning to our lives. Perhaps one of the most painful experiences in life comes from realizing that we have squandered opportunities for appreciating beauty, learning something that interests us, or doing something meaningful for others. Now, there is still time, but Jesus reminds us that the opportunities may not always be there for us. All the more reason to take advantage of them while we can!

Are you content with the way you use your time?

45.

WALKING SECURELY WHEN THE PATHWAY IS DARK.

Jesus said to him, "Do you believe because you see me? How happy are those who believe without seeing me."

John 20:29

Sometimes, believing without seeing is the only way to achieve a desired goal. A good example of this comes from one of my favorite movies, called *The Last Crusade*. It's a story about a man who searches for the Holy Grail, the cup that Jesus used at the Last Supper. After many harrowing experiences, the man discovers the cave in which the cup of Christ is buried. But to reach the cup, he must pass through three final trials. His only help is a book that gives vague hints as to what he must do in order to be successful. He gets through the first two trials, but the last one presents him with an apparent impossibility. In order to get to the Holy Grail, he must cross an incredibly huge gorge. He can't jump over it. It is too wide. He can't climb into it. It is too deep. His only direction from the book is, in so many words, that he must have faith. After fearful hesitation, he tentatively puts his right foot over the gorge, closes his eyes, and takes a step. Immediately a hidden pathway appears that enables him to cross over the gorge. It is this act of faith that wins for him the prize of reaching the Holy Grail.

This story can be taken as a metaphor for the act of faith that enables us to experience the presence of God in our lives. For example, no one "sees" the presence of Jesus in the Eucharist, but our faith in that presence strengthens and comforts us. Jesus promises us resurrected life, but none of us have actually seen its fullness. Jesus promises that he will be present in our lives until the end of the world, but we do not actually see this presence. What we do have is the intuition that Jesus is leading, guiding, and inspiring us. This is something that we sense, and this is the gift that comes as a result of faith. An example of this in my life comes from the experience I have when giving a homily. It is sometimes very difficult to craft a homily, and in the process I wonder if anything worthwhile is going to result from the effort. But I believe that it is through God's inspiration that I am usually able to say something meaningful for others. At least, people tell me that the homilies are meaningful to them. I know that if I have done my part in preparing my ideas, God will make the homily work. In those times when I have forgotten to rely on his help, the homily didn't work. I don't physically see God helping me, but because I have faith in his power, I do experience its effects.

Our faith creates the openness within us that allows the power of God to touch our lives. Faith then is somewhat like giving God permission to act within us. God never forces himself on us, but he offers a friendship and a help that he invites us to accept. It seems to me that faith is our way of accepting this friendship and help, which in this life will always seem somewhat mysterious. Our five senses may not experience God's helping presence, but if we are prayerful, we have intuitions of his power working within our lives. We don't see that power, but we know it through its effects. That is the kind of knowing that flows from a life lived with faith, and we see it as being very real.

Faith enables us to do what we cannot do by ourselves. With faith, we can walk securely when the path is dark. Is your faith strong enough to be a light for your path?

46.
Stay awake!

"Be ready for whatever comes, dressed for action, and with your lamps lit, like servants who are waiting for their master to come back from a wedding feast."

Luke 12:35-36

God comes to us not only at the hour of our death, but many times throughout our lives. Since this is so, Jesus' words about being ready can apply to us in many different ways. We are ready for the coming of God each day when we are awake to the ways in which he speaks to us in the events of our daily lives.

One day I watched an elderly priest sitting on a chair as he threw peanuts to a group of chipmunks. Since he had been doing this for some time, the little animals lost some of their natural fear and gradually came closer to get their fair share. But only one chipmunk trusted enough to come up into the priest's lap, stuff his cheeks with peanuts, and then return for more. Guess who got the lion's share of the peanuts!

Watching this scenario taught me in a concrete way that an act of trust has its rewards. It worked for the chipmunk! And then the thought came to me: How would my life change for the better if I were less fearful and more trusting in God's providence and in his guidance? Would I feel more secure and joyful? I don't believe that God sent that chipmunk to teach me a lesson in trust. But I do believe that God was present within me, enlightening me to make a connection with the chipmunk event that would be meaningful in my relationship with him. Is that what Jesus means when he asks me to be ready, waiting for the master to come? But what if I had not been awake to the inspiration? Or what if I had grasped the meaning and then sloughed it off?

This illustrates a significant example of Jesus' words inviting us to be ready for whatever comes. You never know when an inspiration of God will touch your life. Sometimes God will speak to you through people whose influence enriches you in those times when you need it most. Sometimes his inspirations may come through a book that you happen to find just at the right time. We all need to stay awake to the deeper meanings that ordinary life experiences may hold. God does speak to us through everyday events, and that can have a profound effect in our lives, if we are not asleep.

Are you awake to the ways in which God speaks to you?

47.

GOD'S JUDGMENT IS SIMPLY THE RATIFICATION OF OUR CHOICES.

"If anyone hears my message and does not obey it, I will not judge him. I came not to judge the world, but to save it."
John 12:47

There seems to be a discrepancy about divine judgment as it is presented in Scripture. The text quoted above says that Jesus will not be a judge. But in Matthew 25, Jesus seems to say the opposite. While it is true that the circumstances in the two texts are different, there is still an important question to be asked. In what sense will Jesus evaluate the sum total of the choices we have made in our lives? How will he judge us?

There is a clever cartoon, a part of the Charlie Brown series, in which Lucy is angry because her mother won't allow her to have a birthday party. When her brother Linus asks why, Lucy replies, "Because I've been bad." Linus says, "Well, all you have to do is tell Mother that you're sorry." That sounds good to Lucy, but then she has an afterthought. She looks at Linus and screams, "I'd rather die first." Lucy knew that her bad behavior and lack of repentance would cancel out the birthday party. But she made a decision not to be sorry for her behavior. All that Lucy's mother did was to ratify her decision. That was the judgment.

When we step over the boundaries of space and time, we will see the sum total of all the decisions we have made during our lifetime. Those decisions will lead to a final decision either for or against God. At that point, God will see the decision that we make, and he will allow that decision, with all its consequences, to be in force. That will be the judgment. Our final decision is what causes the judgment. It seems then that the one to fear is not God, but rather, we should fear ourselves.

God created us with free will, and so all through our lives we make choices that are free. We can never make the right ones without God's help and inspiration, but he never takes away our freedom to accept or reject him. All our choices, even the simplest ones, have inescapable consequences. If we have a healthy lifestyle, the consequence will most likely be a delightful sense of well-being. The consequences are quite different if the lifestyle isn't healthy. So it is with our choices for God. God is not a harsh judge, but a loving helper who is constantly giving us the power to reach the joy he wants us to have.

You can never be saved without God, but God leaves you with the power to say "no." We have the tremendous power of choice. Are you satisfied with the choices you've made?

48.
BE CREATIVE IN YOUR LIFE.

Some men came carrying a paralyzed man on a bed, and they tried to carry him into the house and put him in front of Jesus. Because of the crowd, however, they could find no way to take him in. So they carried him up on the roof, made an opening in the tiles, and let him down on his bed into the middle of the group in front of Jesus.

Luke 5:18-19

I don't know how the owner of the house felt about this solution, but you would have to admit that a lot of creativity was involved in making it. The paralytic might not have been healed if his friends had not lowered him through the roof. Jesus responded to their act of faith with the gift of healing, but there would have been no healing at that moment were it not for the creative action of the paralytic's friends. Here is a wonderful example of collaboration between God and men. Divine healing was present in the house, but men had to be creative in finding a way to get to it.

God is present within us and around us, and he desires that we should discover his presence. There is no other way that we can find the fullness of joy that God wills for us to have. Discovering his presence and love more deeply, we enter into an adventure that becomes more enticing as it unfolds each day. But none of us experiences the adventure of knowing God in exactly the same way. Each way has some degree of uniqueness about it, and we have to see what that means as our own adventures unfold. That's where creativity comes in.

We could be creative in the way we pray. Sometimes we can bring new life into our prayer experience by trying new forms. There are many different ways to pray, and reading a good book on prayer could help us to find fresh approaches to deepen our relationship with God. Many people have experienced a deeper relationship with God through the beauty and consolation of centering prayer. You may experience no need or desire to change the way you are praying now. You may have already found what is best for you. But if you feel a need to modify what you are doing, some creativity in exploring other possibilities can unearth treasures that can enrich your prayer life.

We could be creative in the way we participate in the liturgy. Some people complain that, in spite of their best efforts, they find little nourishment in the liturgies they attend. And so they stop attending. But there could be another solution. They could share their needs and ideas within their parish communities. That would be the ideal. If that failed, creativity could entail exploring the possibility of finding liturgies that might better respond to their needs, rather than simply dropping out. I have known people who have benefited from this kind of searching. Their reward was a liturgical experience that brought deeper meaning and new life to their relationship with God.

We could be creative in responding to the needs of our families and communities. We might ask how we could bring more happiness and satisfaction into the lives of those we love. And we could also be more creative in responding to our own needs. This could mean taking more time to relax and enjoy our lives, and taking the necessary quiet time to refresh our minds and hearts.

Creativity in living our lives helps us to make them more fruitful and enjoyable, more open to the discovery of God's presence within and around us. That is what happened to the paralytic, thanks to the caring creativity of his friends. Creativity is certainly a pathway to joy. Is there a part of your life where a more creative approach might be helpful?

49.

WHEN THE LORD KNOCKS, IT PAYS TO OPEN THE DOOR.

"Listen! I stand at the door and knock; if anyone hears my voice and opens the door, I will come into his house and eat with him, and he will eat with me."

Rev. 3:20

Eating together is often a sign in Scripture for the experience of deep sharing and intimate communion. This is the experience that God holds out to us. The Lord knocks at our door, and he invites us to open up to the intimate, loving presence he continually offers to each one of us. When we open the door, we accept the invitation. The initiative is always his. We have only to respond to the knock. Of course this raises an important question: How do we know when the Lord is knocking? How do we perceive that?

Sometimes an experience of God's presence comes to us suddenly and unexpectedly when we are struck by something beautiful in nature. That experience is like a knock on the door of our minds and hearts that invites us to open up and savor his presence as he reveals it through what he has made. We respond by taking time to bask in the awareness, and our openness to the experience gives birth to a feeling of intimacy with God. Something similar can happen when we look at a beautiful work of art or architecture, such as a cathedral. During the five years I spent in Europe, I had many opportunities to stand in awe underneath magnificent stained glass windows and trace their upward sweep toward splendid vaulted ceilings. That experience was like a knock at the door by God that invited me to be silent and receptive, opening myself up to feel something of his transcendence and to commune with it.

This same process is present when we discover a person who reflects moral and spiritual beauty. Such a person is a reflection of God, and the experience entices us to let the reflection into our hearts. And it would be the same for the inspirations that sometimes come to us in prayer. God uses these to knock on the doors of our minds and hearts. When we pay attention and open the doors, something of God's presence enters in, and this creates a joy that brings a delightful meaning into our lives.

God uses many different ways to knock on the door of our lives. If we are too stressed, we may not be able to hear the knocking. When our minds are quiet, we become more aware of the ways God uses to get our attention. Are you aware of the ways God uses to knock on the door of your life?

50.

KNOW YOUR GIFT AND BE THANKFUL.

One and the same Spirit gives faith to one person, while to another person he gives the power to heal. The Spirit gives one person the power to work miracles; to another, the gift of speaking God's message; and to yet another, the ability to tell the difference between gifts that come from the Spirit and those that do not... But it is one and the same Spirit who does all this; as he wishes, he gives a different gift to each person.

I Cor. 12:9-11

Once, while helping out in a parish, I met a gifted priest for whom I had a deep respect. He seemed knowledgeable about many different things, was able to talk intelligently about them, and seemed to be at ease wherever he was. I noticed this and began to wish that I had more of those gifts in my life. Imagine my surprise then when he told someone that he wished he could be more like me. I never fully understood why, but this humorous situation did reveal an important truth to me. Neither of us seemed to be satisfied with the gifts that we had, probably because we were not fully aware of what they were.

No matter how negatively you may sometimes think about yourself, it is really unlikely that God would not have blessed you with at least one gift in your life. It is important for you to know what that is and to appreciate its value. Even if you are bedridden, you still have a gift to offer to others. Your calm acceptance of what cannot be changed will be a powerful message to others, helping them to accept their difficulties with a deeper sense of peace. There are people who have done this for me, and I have learned much from them. Even if you are ill, you can offer your illness and prayers for the sake of others. The offering becomes an energy that touches their lives and gives them the strength they need to do what God wants them to do. All prayer is an energy that you can offer for others, and it will touch their lives in a positive way. This is one of the important messages of the gospel.

Know your gift and be thankful that you can use it to help others. In the acute care and assisted living units where I work, I see a large number of people whose efforts are indispensable for the functioning of those units. Without the housekeeping staff, sanitation would be lacking. Without the dietary staff, residents would not eat. Without the nursing staff, the residents' health would suffer. Without the maintenance staff, the buildings would not be safe. Without the pastoral care staff, spiritual ministration would be lacking. All of these gifts are necessary for the working of the whole. Each individual gift you have is important and necessary, whether that gift is used within a family, in the workplace, or in the community as a whole.

Our lives have a deeper meaning when we know what our gifts are, how they benefit others, and how the gifts of others benefit us. We need to develop our gifts, and to be content with what we have been able to do. Are you aware and thankful for the gifts that are a part of your life?

51.

BE READY FOR SURPRISES.

When Jesus finished telling these parables, he left that place and went back to his hometown. He taught in the synagogue, and those who heard him were amazed. "Where did he get such wisdom?" they asked. "And what about his miracles? Isn't he the carpenter's son? Isn't Mary his mother, and aren't James, Joseph, Simon, and Judas his brothers? Aren't all his sisters living here? Where did he get all this?" And so they rejected him.

Jesus said to them, "A prophet is respected everywhere except in his hometown and by his own family."

Mt. 13:53-57

The people in Jesus' hometown thought that they knew all there was to know about him. Since their minds were not open to anything new, it might have seemed to them that they had nothing new to learn. They were stuck in the past, and so they were closed to the surprise of the present moment. Jesus could do nothing for them, because they were not open to receive the new revelation that he wanted to give them.

Does something similar sometimes happen in our lives? We hear the gospel stories over and over, and perhaps we think to ourselves: Here it is again. I've heard this ever since I was a child. I know what it says. Nothing new here for me! Or we get up in the morning and think, Well, it's going to be another day with the same things that have to be done all over again. Nothing here to look forward to! That may be true if we think the day has nothing to give us. Then we won't recognize the gifts that the day brings, and we won't be open to what it has to offer.

Jesus presented another aspect of himself to the people in his hometown that they had never seen before, but they missed what he offered to them. He gave them something they were not expecting. Perhaps today someone will surprise you with a gesture of friendship or a sign of goodness that you were not expecting. If you are not open to the goodness that life may bring, you may miss the importance of what is being offered. And there may be some new insights waiting for you in the gospel stories that you have heard so often in the past. But you won't know unless you quietly meditate on the words, saying a prayer that the Holy Spirit may show you what they mean for your life. It is true that insights and surprises may not come to us every day. But it is a tragedy if we are not open to them and aware of their importance when they do come.

A good surprise may come your way today. Will you be sufficiently open to recognize it when it comes?

52.

JOY IS THE GIFT KNOWN BY
THE POOR IN SPIRIT.

*Jesus looked at his disciples and said, "Happy are you poor;
the kingdom of God is yours."*

Luke 6:20

At the end of Puccini's opera, *La Boheme*, Mimi is surrounded by her friends as she is dying of tuberculosis. She sings a plaintive aria about the discomfort she feels because her hands are freezing cold. Her friends want to help her, but they are all poor, and they have no money to buy a muffler to keep her hands warm. But they think of a solution. If each one of them sold the one thing he had of value, they could pool their resources and be able to buy the muffler. So this is what each of them does, and in the process of buying the muffler, they become even poorer. But in the process of becoming poorer for the sake of another, they also experience joy.

The poor in spirit know how to prioritize values, how to let go of lesser values for the sake of greater ones. The ability to let go is what enables a person to become poor in spirit, and that ability makes him free. Letting go is a challenge that faces us all of our lives. The choices that faced Mimi's friends are also ours. Letting go enables us to share what we have with others. But the importance of sharing goes beyond financial considerations. You can send a check to your favorite charity, but fail to listen to someone who needs advice, or fail to encourage someone who needs affirmation. People need our time and our energy, and sharing those assets appropriately is perhaps one of the greatest challenges of modern life. If we fail the challenge, we miss our ability to live our lives with joy because we are left only with ourselves. A bit of self-reflection can prove that this is true. Haven't you found more satisfaction in letting go of yourself by sharing with others, than by simply living for yourself?

The poor in spirit know how to give, but paradoxically, they are just as adept in knowing how to receive. They let go of an exaggerated sense of self-sufficiency and accept the truth that colors all of our lives. Each of us has the need to receive from others, even in those areas of life where we think we are strong. Our successes in life never come just from ourselves. They also come through the love and work of many others who have touched our lives in many different ways. When we consider this, we let go of the idea that our achievements flow merely from our own efforts.

Letting go includes much more than the examples we looked at above. The poor in spirit allow their lives to flow freely without grasping onto anything for themselves. They enjoy the gift of the moment, but they refuse to cling to it. They are faithful to their friendships, but they remain open to the ways in which expressions of friendship change. They remain committed to their spiritual life, but they are open to the growth that occurs as their relationship with God deepens. Grasping on to nothing, they are open to all of the growth that the flow of life brings. Such people are the poor in spirit, and truly the kingdom of God is theirs.

Fullness of life belongs to those who are poor in spirit. Where do you need to let go, so that you can be free to grow?

53.

THE TRUTH WILL SET YOU FREE.

So Jesus said to those who believed in him, "If you obey my teaching, you are really my disciples; you will know the truth, and the truth will set you free."

John 8:31-32

Freedom means much more than the ability to go where you want whenever you wish, or to do whatever you want whenever you desire to do it. You could have all of this and still not be free. Take, for example, a person who is addicted to material possessions. He can go where he wants and do what he wants, but still he is not free, because he misses the truth about life. Until he finds that, he cannot find happiness. He remains addicted to a way of looking at life that robs him of meaning, and so he is not free to find the joy that God wants him to have.

The truth of Jesus is that the ultimate meaning in life only comes from a loving relationship with God, along with loving relationships with the whole of God's creation. The truth is that we have a connection to God, to one another, and to everything that is. To recognize the truth is to recognize the connections, and to respond to them with love.

Certain aspects of this truth have recently become the subjects of scientific inquiry, especially in the area of quantum physics. Quantum physics tells us much about the connections that exist in the universe, and how they affect our lives. An excellent resource for this is Ervin Laszlo's book, *Science and the Akashic Field,* which offers a number of examples that show how these connections work. The truth about the universe is that its parts have an effect on one other. It follows that we have deep connections with this universe in which we live, and in a certain sense, we are all part of the whole.

The truth about the universe as explained by quantum physics, and the truth given us by Jesus, have much in common. This, of course, should come as no surprise. The ultimate truth about reality is the same, since it all comes from God. Jesus gives us his truth so that we can live our lives free from illusions that rob us of the happiness God wills us to have. If we live just for ourselves and forget our connections to God and to one another, we lose our freedom to find meaning in our lives. Loving relationships do form the core of meaning for every one of us. Serving God and serving others are ways of life that ultimately bring us joy. This is the truth of who we are. When we understand this, the truth of Jesus really does set us free.

The truth, as Jesus teaches it, is far more than a catalog of religious facts. Jesus' truth is meant to become a living experience, a wellspring that bathes us with meaning. That happens to those who obey his teaching through their love of God and through their love of their brothers and sisters. Those who obey Jesus are the ones who are transformed by what Jesus says. Have you allowed the truth of Jesus to transform you?

54.

HOW TO AVOID UNNECESSARY SUFFERING.

"All of us fell to the ground, and I heard a voice say to me in Hebrew, 'Saul, Saul! Why are you persecuting me? You are hurting yourself by hitting back, like an ox kicking against its owner's stick.'"

Acts 26:14

The voice revealed a healing truth. Paul was hurting himself by fighting against the light of Christ. Until he saw clearly and allowed God to change the direction of his life, he would continue to be lost in a life empty of meaning. This was the unnecessary suffering he endured, the suffering from which God saved him by offering him a new way of life.

It seems to me that at times, most of us are tinged with a kind of darkness that causes us unnecessary suffering. The darkness is often in the form of some sort of addiction that draws us to itself, but in spite of the attraction, it offers us no happiness. On the contrary, it bestows a suffering that steals away the possibility of lasting joy. But in spite of that, we kick against reality and sometimes choose what ultimately can only cause us misery. Years ago I read an example in a book that illustrated how this works. The example dealt with a man who was unfaithful to his wife. Three times a week he had a clandestine meeting with a woman with whom he was having an affair. Each time he did this, he was left with a feeling of disgust and emptiness, but nevertheless, he kept on going back. Now we might ask why he did this, but in the areas of our own addictions, we probably behave in a similar way.

People who overeat know that their habit robs them of good health and causes sluggishness, but they overeat anyway. People who refuse to forgive know that their habit poisons their hearts and destroys their peace of mind, but they refuse to forgive anyway. People who pursue happiness by amassing material goods know that their pursuit eventually becomes boring, but they keep up their pursuit anyway. Trying to find happiness where it cannot be found is like kicking against reality, or in Paul's words, "like an ox kicking against its owner's stick." And kicking against reality is one of the best ways to cause unnecessary suffering.

Perhaps the best way to avoid unnecessary suffering is to pay attention to what works in life and what doesn't; to see what brings joy and meaning and what doesn't. The voice that spoke to Paul told him to stop hurting himself. God's wish for Paul is the same as his wish for us. God wants to free us from unnecessary suffering. If we listen to his words and pay attention to the promptings of his Spirit in our hearts, we can become free of the unnecessary suffering we cause to ourselves. If we accept God's loving power into ourselves, we will have the strength to stop kicking against reality. And what a wonderful experience of joyful freedom that will be!

Are there ways in which you are causing unnecessary suffering to yourself?

55.

GOING BEYOND YOUR FEELINGS.

"Teacher," he asked, "which is the greatest commandment in the Law?" Jesus answered, "'Love the Lord your God with all your heart, with all your soul, and with all your mind.' This is the greatest and the most important commandment. The second most important commandment is like it: 'Love your neighbor as you love yourself.'"

Matthew 22:36-39

Loving another is ultimately the most delightful activity that enlivens our lives. Why then should such a delightful activity be the subject of a commandment? Perhaps the reason is that the feeling of delight comes and goes. It's wonderful when it's there, but just as with every other sensation contained in our repertoire of feelings, you can't count on it to be with you always. The time will come when it leaves you. You may mourn its temporary demise and wonder where it went, but it will always be somewhat of a fickle companion in your journey of life.

Recently I had an interesting conversation with a woman who found it hard to understand how there could be a love without feelings. Finally I thought of an example that could explain this. I asked her to imagine a woman whose husband was mired in infidelity. Eventually when her husband realized the futility of what he was doing, he returned and asked for forgiveness, and a chance to begin again. She made the decision to forgive him, but the love that enabled her to do so would probably be lacking in warm feelings. If she waited for those to develop, she might never be able to forgive him. Perhaps this is why Jesus says to love with all your heart, all your soul, and all your mind. This means that the depth of love needs to go beyond any feelings that may or may not be present. We need to be free to love even when we may not feel like loving. And so we love God when he seems to be absent. We pray even when we seem to get nothing out of it. And we forgive others even when there are no warm feelings to help us along.

If we love only when our love is sustained by good feelings, then we love only for the sake of ourselves. That is why the disappearance of good feelings can sometimes be a grace. When we remain faithful to prayer even when we do not feel like praying, then we love God for himself, rather than for any benefits the love may give to us. And yet, there is an interesting paradox here. The greatest benefits of loving are ours precisely at the moment when we don't seek them. When our minds are directed to those we love rather than to ourselves, we eventually discover a deeper connection with them that otherwise we could not experience. That's what happens when our energy flows outward, rather than getting stuck within ourselves. And that eventually results in a deep sense of fulfillment.

Loving with all your heart, all your soul, and all your mind keeps your energy flowing outward. Jesus' command to love offers us a freedom from the tyranny of feelings, and from getting stuck inside of ourselves. His command is the bedrock on which fidelity and true love can find their support.

True love, like God's love, is steadfast, while a love based on changing feelings is in a state of flux. Which of these two would seem preferable to you?

56.

WHEN YOU DON'T KNOW HOW TO PRAY, ALLOW GOD'S SPIRIT TO GUIDE YOU.

In the same way the Spirit also comes to help us, weak as we are. For we do not know how we ought to pray; the Spirit himself pleads with God for us in groans that words cannot express.

Rom. 8:26

I find great consolation in these words, because sometimes in certain situations I do not know how I ought to pray. For example, if a person is seriously ill, would it be better for him to regain his health, or would it be better for him to be reborn into resurrected life? We cannot know the future, and so we cannot always be sure of what results to pray for. And although we may think that our prayer request will be a blessing if granted, such may not always be the case. This idea forms the plot of W.W. Jacobs' story, *The Monkey's Paw,* and it could be helpful for us to think about its message.

In this short story, a man grabs the monkey's paw and asks for the sum of two hundred British pounds. His wish is granted, but he receives the money as a result of the death of his son, who is fatally crushed in an industrial accident. His next wish is that his son should return back to this life. This wish too is granted, but the son returns in the same horribly mangled form that he had at the moment of his death. Finally the father's only recourse is to wish that his son be definitively taken from this life. That has to become his final wish. The first two wishes seemed good, but they resulted in the opposite of what was really wanted.

Most of our prayer intentions are clearly safe and meaningful, of course, as for example when we pray for the strength to forgive someone, or for the conversion of those who cause harm. We can offer those prayers to God with confidence. The closer we are to God in our mind and hearts, the more likely we are to know how to pray and what to pray for. But we can never know the mind of God completely, and so sometimes our prayers cannot be answered in ways we might wish, or within the particular time frame we might hope for. That is why it seems a good idea to end our petitions with the words Jesus used when he asked to be spared the pains of his passion. He ended his prayer with the words, "Not my will, however, but your will be done." (Luke 22:42) Your will be done! What a wonderful way to pray. We can trust that this prayer will always be answered in God's time, in a way that will be best for us as well as for those for whom we pray.

You can allow God's spirit to guide you in your prayer, because God always wants to bring out the best possible results in whatever situation he finds you. Can you trust God to do that, even when those results do not always seem to make sense?

57.

CLAIM ALL THAT BELONGS TO YOU.

*When the true message, the Good News, first came to you,
you heard about the hope it offers. So your faith and love
are based on what you hope for, which is kept safe for you
in heaven.*

Col. 1:5

The fullness of what we are meant to be has not yet been completely revealed to us, but we hope that one day it will be ours. Paul tells us that what we hope for is being kept safe for us in heaven. Heaven is the name we give to the experience that will be ours when we enter the new life of resurrection. If we die in friendship with God, we will enjoy the fullness of life with him, and it is this life that is kept safe for us in heaven. It is God's gift to us. We can claim it with gratitude and joy.

We can only claim God's gift of resurrected life because he promises it to us, and because God is true to his promises. But since we have free will, God does not force any of his gifts on us. He asks us to make a choice for the gifts that he promises. We can never earn them, because they are given to us freely by God. But we have to accept God's promised gifts with an energetic desire, because otherwise we will have no capacity to enjoy them. Sometimes people find this confusing, because they think that if they live a life in harmony with the gospel, then God has to reward them. And that sounds like they are earning the gift. But consider this example. A child is adopted into a loving family, and obviously he can have no claim that forces the family to adopt him. The adoption is a pure gift. But once the family makes a promise to care for him, then the child can claim the love that the promise entails.

The adopting family certainly wants the child to enjoy the experience of receiving and sharing in the family's love. In order to do this, though, the child has to learn to accept the love, and to share in the family's values. Otherwise, he will feel separated and estranged. All of this is true in our relationship with God. We have to accept his offer and integrate our lives with the values God reveals to us through his word in the Scriptures. Otherwise, there is no shared basis on which the relationship can grow. When we read God's word, we gaze into God's open heart. If we like what we see, we accept the promise of his gift of love, and we live by his values. Then we can claim his love and help in this life, and we can claim the full flowering of God's promises, which are kept safe for us in heaven. We can do this because God is true to the promises he freely makes to us. The initiative is always his, and we can trust where it leads.

God certainly wants you to claim what he is keeping safe for you. How deeply do you believe in the fullness of life that God promises to you?

58.

WE ARE SAFE WITH GOD.

For I am certain that nothing can separate us from his love; neither death nor life, neither angels nor other heavenly rulers or powers, neither the present nor the future, neither the world above nor the world below.

Rom 8:38-39

A friend of mine was almost exhausted by a number of serious problems that had plagued her over a period of several years. One of her children required psychiatric care and had to be sent away for treatment that lasted for several months. Not long after that, another of her many children developed problems that required a period of extensive counseling. A short time later, her husband lost his job with a company that had paid him well over a period of many years. And then, if that were not enough, a fire broke out in their home and did extensive damage. She said that if it had not been for her husband's continuing love, and for their shared faith that God would help them through these sufferings, she never would have survived.

None of these tragedies caused her to cut herself off from her husband's love and support. None of them could separate her from her love of God. We could ask why all of these difficulties had to happen, but of course there would be no absolutely clear answer. The important point is that in the midst of these tragedies my friend made a choice to remain connected to her husband's love and committed to her trust in God's love for her. With them, she was safe.

This story does have a happy ending. Most of the tragedies were resolved. Her close relationship with her husband, and her loving trust in God, continued to grow. This was the result of her free decision. Not everyone who experiences tragedies comes through them as successfully as my friend did. I have seen marriages break up because of financial difficulties, or because of problems caused by illness. I have seen people become bitter and lose faith in God when tragedies struck their lives. It seems that in the midst of our personal difficulties we have some degree of choice as to how we will respond. We may need help from wise friends and professional counselors as we struggle with our options, but ultimately, the choice is ours. My friend's choice was a contemporary realization of the beautiful idea of Romans 8 as quoted above. There is a powerful message here for us. When life's burdens become heavy, we may find it difficult at times to put that message into practice. But if we choose to be prayerful, we discover the guidance and power of God, who gently leads us through all the difficulties of our lives.

No tragedy can separate us from the love of God. These are the hopeful words that we find in Romans 8. Do you allow them to take root in your life?

59.

IF YOU WANT TO EXPERIENCE JOY, BRING JOY TO OTHERS.

"The measure you use for others is the one that God will use for you."

Luke 6:38

One of the great tragedies of our individualistic society is our failure to appreciate sufficiently our connections to one another. Our actions have an effect on others, just as the actions of others have an effect on us, whether we realize it or not. And of course our actions have an effect on ourselves. We cannot escape these effects. If we do good to others, we usually experience a sense of joy and harmony within ourselves. This is the way God made us to be. In this sense, the measure we use for others is the one that comes back to rest on us. The reason for this is that we are all connected to one another, and so what we do to others will naturally have an effect on us. That effect is willed by God as a result of the way he made things to be. It is present in all phases of our lives.

We experience daily the influence that the various parts of our bodies have on one another. The health or illness of one part affects all the others. Biological and medical literature emphasize this point. And in our families and societies, we can clearly see the effects that people have on one another by what they say and do. Sociological and psychological literature emphasize this point. What can we say, then, about the effects of our spiritual attitudes on one another? The Bible and the writings of spiritual masters enlighten us on this point.

A spirituality that stresses the importance of loving others is not built on dreamy ideas or on a piety that has little basis in reality. Rather, it is built on the way reality works. The more we are in tune with the connections uniting all things, the more we are in tune with the way things are. Eat intelligently, and health will be measured out to you, because there is a connection between good nourishment and good health. That's reality. Act unselfishly with love, and joy will be measured out to you, because there is a connection between loving others and the experience of joy. That too is reality. The more we are in tune with reality, the more we will enjoy the satisfaction in life that God wills us to have.

If life doesn't seem to measure out much joy to you, ask yourself how much joy you are measuring out to others.

60.

How to become successful.

"Whoever makes himself great will be humbled, and whoever humbles himself will be made great."

Mt. 23:12

This statement of Jesus may seem paradoxical, but it does illustrate a basic truth about human life that offers success and joy. Consider the following example.

Years ago when I was on the administrative staff of a medical center in Gary, Indiana, a decision was made to ask employees for ideas on how to improve the medical center's services. People with MBAs sat down with those who had only finished high school and asked for their suggestions. There was a time when some managers with business degrees thought that they could solve most problems on their own. But many managers today have discovered that things run more smoothly when they tap into the experience of ordinary employees. When managers rely only on their own position, they run the danger of being humbled. When managers reach out to their subordinates and learn from them, they are more likely to be successful and admired for their accomplishments.

The value of humility is valid for all the aspects of our lives. Arrogant people who lack respect for the value of others eventually discover that others will not respect them. And that will be a humbling experience for the arrogant. People who think they can live successfully without God's help will experience psychological and moral difficulties that they won't be able to handle. And that will be a humbling experience for the self-sufficient.

Humility is born from the realization that our success in life comes not just from our own efforts, but also from the help of many who play a part in our lives. Humility, then, is our ability to acknowledge the truth about our lives and to be grateful for what we receive. It is an attitude that wins the cooperation and respect of others.

It would seem that only the truly humble can become truly successful. Would that statement make sense in your life?

61.

ACCEPT LIFE FAITHFULLY, NO MATTER WHERE IT LEADS.

Jesus took the twelve disciples aside and said to them, "Listen! We are going to Jerusalem where everything the prophets wrote about the Son of Man will come true. He will be handed over to the Gentiles, who will make fun of him, insult him, and spit on him. They will whip him and kill him, but three days later he will rise to life."

Luke 18:31-33

A brother in our infirmary once asked me, "Why did God allow his Son to suffer so much? How could he allow him to be crucified?" These are disturbing questions, but we can say that the crucifixion was the result of human iniquity, the refusal of people to accept the revelation of Jesus. In the face of that reality, what the Father asked of his Son Jesus is similar to what he asks of us: to live faithfully and lovingly in the circumstances that life brings, and to accept what we cannot change.

Jesus was incarnated into our midst in order to reveal to us the mind and heart of the One who sent him. Those who accepted the revelation and lived according to it would be animated by the loving presence of God, both in this life and in the life to come. In other words, they would be saved. Those who rejected God's revelation would lose their chance for happiness. The choice was theirs. But their choice affected not only their own lives, but also the life of Jesus. Their rejection ultimately became the cause of his crucifixion. That was the circumstance in his life that Jesus accepted.

It was clear to Jesus that, if he were to remain true to his mission to reveal the mind and heart of the Father, his fidelity would result in his death. He experienced his contemporaries' rejections and knew where they would lead. Yet Jesus freely accepted these unavoidable circumstances in his life, because the most important reality for Jesus was fidelity to his mission. This fidelity was the will of the Father. Jesus' fidelity saved us. We would hardly have been obedient to his word and trustful of his promises if Jesus had not been faithful to his mission.

Jesus was willing to accept the flow of his life, no matter where it would lead him. And he was willing to accept the circumstances of his life that he could not change, even though that led to death on a cross. He did this for us. Here we have the proof of God's love, a love that remains true no matter what circumstances may arise. It is a love that turns death into a new life of resurrection. This is what happened to Jesus, and this is what will happen to us if we are faithful.

May we do in our lives what Jesus did in his: living the demands of life faithfully even when circumstances make that difficult. This is the pathway of life that leads to the resurrection.

What would you need to change in order to follow Jesus more faithfully?

62.

WHY THE RESURRECTED LIFE WILL BE THE FULFILLMENT OF YOUR DREAMS.

What no one ever saw or heard, what no one ever thought could happen, is the very thing God prepared for those who love him.

1 Cor 2:9

Thirty people had just gathered together for a weekend retreat, and for their first meeting, the retreat director posed the following scenario. "Imagine," he said, "that you are on the top of a forty-story building, and there's a plank that leads to the top of the building across the alley. If you cross over, you can have anything you want as a reward. What would it take to get you to walk across that plank, forty stories high, to the other side?" There was a moment of silence, and then one of the retreatants raised his hand. "I would walk across that plank," he said, "if I knew that there would be someone on the other side who would love me."

The retreatant wanted what we all want. Ultimately, we want to love and to know that we are loved. We want to experience the presence and intimate love of God without the fear that we might lose it. We want to belong to a community where there is a sharing of knowledge and mutual acceptance. We want to contemplate the beauty of those who are important to us, and to grow in our understanding of them in friendships that will never end. In short, we long for heaven, for the resurrected life. It is only in the resurrected life, beyond space and time, that we will have the conscious capacity to realize the fulfillment of all these desires. Our fulfillment comes to its full flowering when we cross over the plank from this life to the life of resurrection. Then there will be no suffering to diminish the full flowering of life, and no death to destroy life's promise.

The way we experience resurrected life will be determined by our personalities. We will experience God, the universe, and one another in different ways. An artist will experience the universe in a way that differs from a philosopher or a mathematician. But because we are all bound together in God through love, we will be able to learn from one another, as we do in this life. We will be able to integrate the experiences and insights of others into our own experiences and insights. And so our ability to grow in appreciating God and all of his creation will be practically without limit.

According to contemporary field physics, connections between entities exist throughout the universe. These connections continue to touch our lives even when we are reborn into the life of resurrection, and they contribute to our fulfillment and joy. One of my greatest joys is to receive new insights about life through the writings of spiritual authors, and also from scientists who show the compatibility between recent scientific discoveries and religious belief. I add to that all that I learn from the spiritual experience and insights of my friends. This contributes immensely to my joy. As wonderful as this is, it pales in comparison to the joys of communication among those who share in the resurrected life. Then, all the obstacles to communication and love that we experience in this life will be wiped away. The selfishness that often blinds us will be gone. Truly, that will be the fulfillment of our dreams.

This life is good, but the best is yet to come. Our capacity to love and to know will burst through the limits of space and time and find its full flowering in eternity. This is God's wonderful gift. Is there anything greater than this that he could have given to you?

63.

GOD SHOWS HIS LOVE FOR US THROUGH SIGNS.

"Whoever eats my flesh and drinks my blood has eternal life, and I will raise him to life on the last day."

John 6:54

A person who cares deeply for another will often give a tangible sign to express his love. A simple hug, loving words, a bouquet of roses, or some other thoughtfully chosen gift—all of these are signs that show love. Without signs, we can't tell if we are loved.

Jesus understood our human need for signs, and so he gave us the Eucharist. The Eucharist is a primary sign from God that says, "I care for you. I love you." But that, as beautiful as it is, is not enough for God. The consecrated bread and wine are not only signs of love, but also they are the real sacramental presence of Jesus in our midst. Whenever we receive the consecrated host, and whenever we drink the consecrated wine, we are touching God. One can also say, of course, that we are at the same time being touched by God. What a beautiful expression of divine intimacy! Intimacy beautifully summarizes what God's will is for us. In fact, one could say that intimacy is God's essential way of relating to us. The Eucharist is a sign and reality of that intimacy, and it reflects the mind and heart of God, who offers intimacy to us at each moment of our day. There is never a moment when God is not present to us, and so the Eucharist reflects what always is, and what is always meant to be. We can become aware of this relationship at any time we choose. A good example of this would be the experience of couples who enjoy a successful marriage. They celebrate anniversaries and share tokens that are special signs of the love they have for one another. But those special signs signify a love that is always there. And they can become aware of that love whenever they choose to do so.

While the Eucharist is a preeminent way in which God reveals his love, it does not diminish the importance of myriads of other signs that announce his presence. The entire creation is a sign of God's presence and love. Patterns of order that pervade all parts of the universe reflect the intelligent love of the Creator who caused them to be. Even much of the universe's seemingly random activity reveals an order that goes beyond the postulation of chance. As beautiful as this is, it cannot match the sign of human love and fidelity that reflects God's revelation of who he is for us. Wherever we see the signs of genuine human love, we see a dim reflection of the way God loves.

Just as people give signs of caring to those they love, so God gives signs to those he loves. Love and signs go together. The signs of love are there for all of us. Are you sufficiently awake to see those signs in your life?

64.

THERE IS NO ONE TO GO TO BESIDES GOD.

So he asked the twelve disciples, "And you—would you also like to leave?" Simon Peter answered him, "Lord, to whom would we go? You have the words that give eternal life."
John 6:67-68

Jesus had just told the crowd that unless they ate his flesh and drank his blood, they would not have life in them. Not surprisingly, many walked away. Peter was faced with the same mystery as those who left, but he chose to stay. Peter had heard Jesus' message and had seen his miracles. His heart told him that, although he was now faced with an incomprehensible mystery, he had no one to go to except Jesus.

Like Peter, we too are faced with our own forms of incomprehensible mysteries. An accident takes the life of someone we love. An extended illness changes our lives in ways that seem horrendous. We look at these and similar experiences, and we cannot make sense out of them. We may be tempted to walk away from Jesus. In moments like these, we can pray for the strength to imitate Peter's response. For we too have heard God's message and experienced his goodness in so many ways. And so our hearts tell us, we have no one else to go to except Jesus.

Our belief in the uniqueness of Jesus is nourished by our communication with him in prayer. It seems to me that without prayerful communication, we never come to know who Jesus is for us. When you spend quality time with someone, you gradually experience the importance of that person in your life, and you trust the relationship in spite of the enigmas that always seem to be a part of human love. The following story illustrates this point beautifully.

The story begins with a couple whose marriage appears to be healthy and whose lives flow along peacefully without serious problems. But as the story unfolds, puzzling events soon start to take place. The husband begins to receive strange phone calls in the middle of the night, and sometimes he leaves home without any explanation of why he has to go. Finally, his wife confronts him. "Is there another woman?" she asks. "No," he replies. "There is no other woman. I can't tell you now why I have to do what I am doing, but very soon everything will be clear to you. Please, just trust me." That becomes more difficult because as the story develops, he is accused of being a Communist spy. His family disowns him, but his wife still believes that there will be an explanation for this terrible enigma. And she is right. The story ends with a courtroom scene, in which he reveals that he is a double agent, working for the United States government. At that moment, everything becomes clear.

Why did the man's wife trust him when no one else did? Her faith seemed to be based on her perception of his goodness. When you love someone, you reflect often on who that person is, and you come to know whether or not he is trustworthy. In his wife's view, this man was a person who loved faithfully, and who had a personality that had been trustworthy. Her overall experience of him overrode the doubts caused by his enigmatic behavior, and so when he asked for her trust, she was able to give it.

A person who knows God by reflecting on his word and communicating with him through prayer comes to know his goodness. And so in the midst of life's unsettling enigmas, he has a basic intuition that allows him to trust God. I think this cannot happen without a life of some reflection and prayer. Without these, one cannot have faith in the goodness of God's loving presence in his life. Faith, of course, is God's gift. Prayerful communication with God enables us to accept the gift and to say with Peter, "Lord, to whom would we go? You have the words that give eternal life."

The New Testament shows how Peter's faith brought meaning and increasing clarity to his life. Can you hope that your faith will do the same for you?

65.

THE VALUE OF LEARNING HOW TO LET GO.

Another man said, "I will follow you, sir; but first let me go and say good-bye to my family." Jesus said to him, "Anyone who starts to plow and then keeps looking back is of no use for the Kingdom of God."

Luke 9:60-62

Jesus' words seem at first glance to be somewhat cold. If you leave people who care about you and you do not tell them that you are going away, that would seem to show a lack of love. But that is not the issue here. So perhaps we could look for a deeper meaning in Jesus' statement. Jesus' words are a prophetic invitation to examine how we need to let go of the past, so that we can become freer to do God's will in the present.

The attitude of letting go applies not only to attachments to material things. It also includes being free from various preoccupations that interfere with what God calls us to do. Jesus' words invite us to live attentively in the present moment, and to see the opportunities that lie within it. You can see how this works in the above gospel story, where Jesus invited a man to do something new. Jesus presented him with a wonderful opportunity to change his life and the lives of others by following him in a new way. However, the man was sidetracked by other concerns. The point was not that the other concerns should be ignored or forgotten. But at the moment he called this man, Jesus was asking him for a total immersion in the present. He wanted him to focus on the meaning of his call that would change his life, and to be aware of the beauty and importance of what he was being called to do. Jesus was inviting him to let go of the past, insofar as the past stood in the way of what was needed in the present. This is the invitation Jesus gives to each of us. We need to ask ourselves what we are holding on to, and what preoccupations keep us from following the inspirations that God puts into our hearts. Our happiness will depend on how well we are willing to let go of those preoccupations.

God's will for us is that we should be fully alive, becoming fully what he inspires us to be in the present moment. That may include greater responsiveness to the needs of others, or active concern for the protection of our environment, or more time for quiet meditation so that we can be aware of God's inspirations. These are all examples of what it means to follow Jesus. The path will be somewhat different for each one of us, and yet in the deepest sense it will be the same. We are all called to love as Jesus tells us to love, to be in union with God and with one another both in our minds and in our hearts. But we will realize this union in different ways, depending on our personalities and the circumstances in which we live. And, like the man in the gospel story, we will need to let go of the obstacles and preoccupations that keep us from following our path.

Letting go is not a task that we can do by ourselves. Success comes from God's power working within us. How often do you ask God to help you become free?

66.
BUILD YOUR HOUSE ON ROCK.

"So then, anyone who hears these words of mine and obeys them is like a wise man who built his house on rock. The rain poured down, the rivers flooded over, and the wind blew hard against that house. But it did not fall, because it was built on rock."

Mt. 7:24-25.

You and I have something in common. We have all received the words of Jesus, which reveal to us the mind and heart of God. We can build our lives on his words with confidence, believing they lead to the love and peace that we long to experience within ourselves and with others. But Jesus' words can only become the rock-like foundation of our lives if we take time to reflect on their meaning.

When something is important in our lives, we usually know how to find time for it. Whether it is sports, a favorite television program, a physical fitness program, or keeping in touch with friends, we make sure that our attractions are not forgotten. And so it seems that we could find time for a bit of reflection on the meanings that the words of Jesus have for us. The major consideration would not be the availability of time, but rather the presence of desire. And it may be that the desire takes over only when we start with an act of faith. We begin to read and reflect on Jesus' words, hoping that they will influence, enrich, and change our lives. As we persevere in our reflections, we discover that what we hoped for is actually taking place. And discovery is what enkindles our desire for continued reflection. Would this work for you? You can only find out by testing the process. Here is a good way to do that.

Read the gospel slowly, until you find a passage that captures your attention. Let us suppose that you come across Jesus' words about the wise man who built his house on rock. A part of that text is at the beginning of this section. After reading the passage, you stop and reflect for a few moments on what these words of Jesus mean to you. You could turn your reflection into a short prayer in which you talk with Jesus about the way you are building your life. Is it built on rock or on sand? If it seems that you are building on rock, you might want to give thanks for the power of God, who enables you to be a successful builder. On the other hand, if you seem to be building on sand, you might ask what needs to be changed. When you finish your reflection, sit silently and allow God to speak to you through the inspiration of the Holy Spirit. The silence is crucial, because God's guidance can best be sensed when the mind is quiet. Do not be in a hurry to move out of this period of quiet receptivity.

This is not an exercise where you read many chapters of the Bible at one sitting. That can be done at another time. For this exercise, you read only for a few moments until you find a passage that captures your attention. Then you prayerfully reflect on the passage. If the passage depicts an action, for example the scene in which Jesus first calls his apostles, you might imagine yourself present there. What does it feel like to be called? How does Jesus call you? After a period of prayerful dialog, follow with a period of silence in which you listen for God's guidance. This is particularly important, so it will be vital to spend sufficient time in the silence. When you sense the need to move on, continue your reading for a short time until you find another passage that captures your attention and then continue with a reflection and a period of silence. This is an exercise that helps you to discover the meaning of Jesus' words as they apply to you now. If you build your life on what you discover, then truly you are building your life on rock.

How often do you take the time to reflect on the meaning of Jesus' words as the foundation for the building of your life?

67.

LIFE IS MEANT TO BE ENJOYED.

"When the Son of Man came, he ate and drank, and everyone said, 'Look at this man! He is a glutton and wine drinker, a friend of tax collectors and other outcasts.' God's wisdom, however, is shown to be true by its results."

Mt. 11:19

It seems that Jesus knew how to appreciate the good things of life. Unfortunately, some of his contemporaries used this to discredit him, just as they discredited John the Baptist for doing the opposite. John fasted and drank no wine. One could say that some people will be unhappy with you no matter what you do, but it seems important to note that Jesus enjoyed food and wine, and as other parts of the Bible tell us, he was aware of the beauty of nature. There are also indications that Jesus had friends and that he spent time with them.

We become healthier and more joyful to the extent that we emulate these attitudes of Jesus toward life. But you might think, aren't most of us already doing that? Well, perhaps not as much as you might suppose! Some time ago I saw a cartoon showing a man on vacation at a beautiful beach. But instead of enjoying all of the natural beauty and relaxing in the midst of it, he was on his cell phone, checking up on his business, and worrying about how things were going back home. Only a part of him was at the beach. Another part of him was somewhere else. How often are we really present to what we should be enjoying? How many times are our bodies in one place while our minds are in another?

All of creation is God's gift to us. Surely God must want us to notice it, appreciate it, and enjoy what he has given. In fact, we would be ungrateful if we paid no attention to the gift. That would be like a person who receives a carefully chosen present from a friend, gives it a cursory glance, and then shoves it back into its box. I actually saw this happen once, and I was amazed at what seemed to be a thoughtless indifference. Gifts should be appreciated and enjoyed.

We know we are loved when we see the many gifts of creation God has given to us. The more awake we are to them, the more we respond to the love. That was the attitude of Jesus. Are you fully awake to the gifts you have received?

68.

YOU WILL ALWAYS BE UNIQUE AND SPECIAL IN THE EYES OF GOD.

The Lord said to me, "I chose you before I gave you life, and before you were born I selected you to be a prophet to the nations."

Jeremiah 1:5

Jeremiah had a special place in God's plans for his people, and we can still admire today all of the things God achieved through him. Is it true, though, that only people like Jeremiah should be regarded as special in God's eyes? Suppose that you changed these words so that they applied to the particular circumstances of your life. Could you say, then, that God chose you to bring comfort to the people you have helped? Could you say that God chose you to raise the children he intended for you to have, or that he chose you for the particular career that would affect the lives of others? In all of these circumstances, only you could have the special effect on others that your life was able to give. That is the unique quality of your life.

We are special in the eyes of God not only for what we do, but also for who we are. Before we are chosen to do anything, we are first chosen just to be. In the quotation cited above, God tells Jeremiah that he chose him before he gave him life. In other words, God loved Jeremiah before he accomplished any of the things for which he would be remembered. That gives us a clue as to how God regards us. We are loved even if we fail at what we do, or even if we are ill and unable to do anything at all. This is one of the main messages of the Bible, and it is unfortunate that so many of us have difficulty in accepting it.

The gift of being special is not just yours alone. It belongs to everyone who exists. God has a purpose for everyone to whom he gives life, and he loves each one for who he or she is. If we want to imitate God, we will try to see others as God sees them. And then, we will recognize and respect each person's special quality of beauty and worth. Looking at others in this way is a benefit to ourselves, because recognizing goodness can generate a sense of joy.

There are, of course, egotistical ways of looking at ourselves as special. That happens when we forget that whatever good we have, we have received from God. And we become mired in egoism when preoccupation with our gifts blinds us to the fact that others are gifted too. But we see ourselves appropriately when we recognize that what makes us special comes as God's gift. Is this the way you see yourself?

69.

SUCCESS BELONGS TO THOSE WHO PERSEVERE AND STAND FIRM.

"Everyone will hate you because of me. But not a single hair from your heads will be lost. Stand firm, and you will save yourselves."

Luke 21:17-19

These words remind me of the martyrs who so courageously gave their lives as a testimony to their belief in Jesus. Thanks to the power of Jesus at work within them, they stood firm in times of adversity. They not only found ultimate meaning in their lives through their fidelity, but they also became examples of courage for us. At times, I have questioned whether or not I would be able to stand firm in the face of hatred and death as they did. How would you answer that question if you asked it of yourself? The answer should come not from what you think you might do, but rather from what you believe God would do. The power to stand firm comes from God. You and I need the unwavering faith to believe that God will give us that power when we find ourselves in situations that leave us powerless.

You may never have to face the challenge of martyrdom, but standing firm is an empowering attitude that will help you to deal with all of life's challenges, whatever they may be. You may have to become a caregiver for a loved one who has a long-term illness, and your energies may be stretched to the limit. Someone you love may abandon you, and it may take a long time before you recover from the pain. You may lose your independence through a physical disability that requires you to rely on others for your care. These are just a few of life's problems that cannot always be avoided. Avoid the problems that you can, but when you are faced with the unavoidable, trust in God's power to help you stand firm.

Success in standing firm grows when we believe in God's promise that he is with us in our suffering, and that suffering is never the last word about our lives. That promise gives us the courage to be steadfast in enduring those difficult situations that we cannot escape in the present moment. But there is more, because God's promise says something wonderful about our life in the future. Jesus' resurrection showed us that we are destined for a life where there will be no more suffering. The final word about our lives will be an unimaginable joy in which we will be fully healed, and fully at one with God and with one another. It is for this joy that we were born. If we had no hope in this joy, would we have the courage to be steadfast in the midst of the difficulties that often swirl around us?

Jesus tells us to stand firm. We do that through our belief that he helps us in this present moment. And we are sustained through our hope in a future where suffering will no longer have any place. Belief and hope are truly choices that lead to joy. Is your life inspired by these choices?

70.
REMEMBER WHAT YOU LOOK LIKE.

Whoever listens to the word but does not put it into practice is like a man who looks in a mirror and sees himself as he is. He takes a good look at himself and then goes away and at once forgets what he looks like.

James 1:23-24

If the way you look is unimportant to you, you probably won't pay much attention to what you see in the mirror. It would be unfortunate, though, if inattention to your appearance were so pronounced that you became an eyesore to others. The text quoted above is not concerned with physical appearances, though. It is a metaphor for what takes place in us when we forget what we look like spiritually. That can happen when God's word loses its influence in the way we live. Then our spiritual condition becomes unimportant to us, and we forget who we are meant to be.

There is only one way in which you and I can experience the word of God in our minds and hearts. We have to live the word. If we do not put the word into practice, we hear it and then forget what we heard. Then the word never becomes a part of our lives, and it cannot bear fruit within us. We become out of step with God and with those who live God's word. At times we may not even be aware that this is happening to us, because we do not always have a clear insight as to how we look in the spiritual dimensions of our lives.

In order to become conscious of our relationship with God, we need to take a courageous look at who we really are. We gaze into God's open heart by pondering his word, and then we look within ourselves to see how well we make that word a part of our lives. We could imagine that our lives are like a huge garden. Parts of the garden are well cared for, cultivated, watered, and full of flowers that are breathtakingly beautiful.

Other parts of the garden are neglected and full of weeds. This could well be an apt metaphor for our lives, and we could ask what causes the weeds to grow, and what we might do to clear them out. If we make time for some periods of quiet introspection in our lives, the answers will slowly come into focus. We might discover where the weeds are, and where we need to be more open to God's word so that it can work its life-giving powers within us. But we would also come to know more deeply the good that God has enabled us to achieve. If we do this often enough, we will not forget who we are. We will remember to be thankful for the good within us, while remembering at the same time to ask for healing in those areas where we need it.

God opens his heart to us so that we might know and love him. His word reveals to us who he is and who we are meant to be. When we accept his word and live it, our minds and hearts become a mirror of the power of God working within us. How often do you take time to look into the mirror? Do you like what you see?

71.
LOVE GOD WILDLY.

Then Mary took a whole pint of a very expensive perfume made of pure nard, poured it on Jesus' feet, and wiped them with her hair. The sweet smell of the perfume filled the whole house. One of Jesus' disciples, Judas Iscariot—the one who was going to betray him—said, "Why wasn't this perfume sold for three hundred silver coins and the money given to the poor?" But Jesus said, "Leave her alone! Let her keep what she has for the day of my burial. You will always have poor people with you, but you will not always have me."

John 12:3-6, 7-8.

Judas had a point. It might have seemed more logical to sell the perfume for the benefit of the poor. But Mary operated from a different level of awareness, the level of ecstatic love, and that level has its own brand of logic. If we have ever loved deeply in life, we can understand why Mary felt compelled to pour out the expensive perfume over Jesus' feet. Remember a time when you loved someone with all your heart. There was nothing that you would not have done for that person. Perhaps some of your actions might have seemed strange to others, but because of your intense degree of love, they made perfect sense to you. Your whole being was absorbed into that experience of love, and you would have denied nothing to the one who captured your heart.

Perhaps the same could be said for someone who is totally captivated by an ideal in life, or by a particular career. I remember the story of a freshman at Notre Dame who walked around squeezing a ball in his hand day after day. When asked why he did that, he said, "I am getting myself ready to be a surgeon." People spend years getting ready for a profession or a hobby that becomes totally absorbing to them. Mountain climbers sometimes put up with tremendous inconvenience and tiring exertion just to get to the top. Serious athletes would understand this kind of commitment.

A tremendous amount of absorbing dedication exists in the lives of those who are driven by love or by an ideal. And then there are those who are driven by the love of God, as in the case of Mary, who poured out expensive perfume on the feet of Jesus. To love God in this way is a great gift, because it gives an ultimate meaning to our lives that is totally fulfilling. We are made for this love, even though we may fall short of the dedication that moved Mary as she poured out her precious perfume. Her love was marked by an enthusiastic extravagance that perhaps we have not been able to match. But we can pray daily for the gift to love God unselfishly, with as much energy as we are able to muster. We can't do this by ourselves. It will come as a result of God's spirit working within us. But if God is love, as the Bible often states, then love is God's will for us, for he wants our hearts to beat as one. He will certainly answer us if we pray for the gift to be able to love him to the fullness of our ability.

Love saves us from the sterility of being locked up within ourselves. Love leads us to the experience of oneness with the one we love. Nothing can be more meaningful or delightful than this. How often do you pray for the gift to be able to love God with all of your mind, heart, and soul?

72.

SEE THE WORLD AS GOD DOES.

After John had been put in prison, Jesus went to Galilee and preached the Good News from God. "The right time has come," he said, "and the Kingdom of God is near! Turn away from your sins and believe the Good News!"

Mark 1:14-15

The Good News is that God is completely and totally in love with us, and indeed, with all of creation. Everything else about the Good News flows from this one central reality. A refusal to believe in this love of God for us and for all that he has made would be a refusal to see the world as God sees it. That would be our greatest sin. But we could fall short in still another way. We might give lip service to a belief in God's love, but then simply shrug it off with an attitude of indifference. If we realized what we were doing, then that too would be a sin, because we would be closing ourselves off from God's love and its transforming power in our lives. And so Jesus tells us to turn away from our sins and to believe in the Good News he comes to give us. He asks us to see the world as God sees it.

If God loves us, then by that very fact, we ourselves become loveable. It should not be surprising that God sees the whole world as loveable. He created it, and therefore it reflects something of who God is, just as the work of an artist will reflect something of who the artist is.

And so our joyful task is to see the world through God's eyes and to respond to it as he does. I think that this task begins as a contemplative one. God ponders the goodness of what he has made, and it would seem that we need to imitate him in his pondering. When we love someone deeply, we think about that person often, and so we come to know the beauty that our loved one reflects to us. How deeply our lives would be enriched if we became more aware of the beauty of all God's creation, if we could love and see it as God loves and sees it. Would such a vision also have an effect on the way we care for one another, as well as for our environment, which so greatly needs our care and respect?

As Jesus tells us in the above quote from Mark, "The right time has come." Now is the time to accept the Good News and to see the world as God sees it. What a wonderful pathway to a deeper sense of meaning and a fuller experience of joy. If we want more of that, this is the right time to pray that God's vision of life will become ours. Are you ready to fully open your heart and be changed by the Good News?

73.

BE CONTENT TO LIVE WITH MYSTERY.

Jesus went on to say, "The Kingdom of God is like this. A man scatters seed in his field. He sleeps at night, is up and about during the day, and all the while the seeds are sprouting and growing. Yet he does not know how it happens."

Mark 4:26-27

We know more about the biological mechanism of sprouting seeds than Jesus' contemporaries did, but even for us the process is wrapped in an aura of mystery. From a small seed comes a plant that nourishes us, while at the same time it produces many other seeds that will continue to bring new life. We might wonder how one small seed can do all of this. Surely this mystery is a gift of God. And yet this is only the tip of the iceberg that reminds us of the many other mysteries we encounter in life.

One of the most profound mysteries I experienced was when I tried to prepare a homily for my mother's funeral. I have always found it rather easy to give a homily when celebrating a funeral Mass, or a Mass of Resurrection as it is more fittingly called today. I believe so much in God's promise of resurrection that the thoughts I want to share seem to flow automatically. But when my mother died, no thoughts came to me. As I tried to prepare a homily, all I could do was sit in a numbing daze. Finally I offered a prayer, and part of that prayer was a petition to my mother—"Mom, what do you want me to say?" And I felt within me an answer that said, "Why don't you just tell them about the enjoyment I am experiencing now?" Immediately the words flowed out, and the whole homily came in a flash. I was able to share some ideas of what the resurrected life might be like, and those who heard them told me later how meaningful those ideas were to them. So where did the words come from? Just like the mystery of the seed, this too was a mystery that was a gift from God.

Perhaps something similar happened to you when you needed to find the right words to help someone who came to you with a problem. You had no idea of what to say, but the right words came just at the moment when they were needed. Again, a mystery! Again, a gift from God!

Then, of course, there are the cosmic mysteries that we can never explain. For example, the universe only exists in its present form because of the exquisite balance of the force of gravity with the other forces governing the universe. If gravity's force had been just a slight bit stronger, the universe would have collapsed inward upon itself. If the force had been just a slight bit weaker, the stars and planets would never have been able to form. But the force was just right. Again, a mystery! Again, a gift from God!

Years ago I came across a saying that read like this: Is life a problem to be solved, or a mystery to be lived? We are immersed in many mysteries that we cannot completely understand, but they are all gifts of God that enhance our lives, and even make them possible. Can you appreciate the mysteries that make up your life, and see them as gifts of God to you?

74.

SERVE WITH A WILLING AND JOYFUL HEART.

Each one should give, then, as he has decided, not with regret or out of a sense of duty; for God loves the one who gives gladly.

2 Cor. 9:7

I have always been impressed by those who care for the ill with a smile on their faces, and with a love that seems to inspire what they do. They bring joy to others and in doing so, they discover a sense of fulfillment for themselves. But I have met a few people who served the ill not with a smile, but with a scowl, and one of them admitted that her only motivation was a paycheck. Such people miss something very important in their lives. They miss the satisfaction of bringing joy to others.

Most of us have some responsibility for others, either because of family obligations or because of the work that we have chosen to do. We also have a responsibility for the poor, an obligation to share our resources with them to the extent that we are able. We can fulfill these responsibilities out of a sense of duty, or out of a sense of love. It would seem that our journey along the pathway of life becomes more enjoyable to the extent that we give to others with love and with concern for their well-being. Of course, we can give to one another simply because we are forced to, much in the way that we might pay our income tax on April 15th. But there would be no sense of fulfillment in that, no sense of joy. In fact, a loveless life is the greatest cause of boredom.

When God sent his Son to live among us, he came with a willing and joyful heart. He was motivated by love, and not by a sense of dry duty. All that Jesus said and did simply reflected the love that he felt for us. When we serve with a willing and joyful heart, we imitate Jesus, and we show to others what their lives can be like. I have learned much by observing those who serve the sick with love and care. They have shown me what my life can be like, and how I might live with a greater awareness of what others need from me. It seems, then, that we can accomplish much if we serve others with a willing and joyful heart. That is how we bring joy to those we serve in our families and communities.

What about those of us who are ill and infirm, those who are no longer capable of being responsible for others? If we are ill, we can appreciate the care we receive and express gratitude for it. People want to be appreciated. When we express gratitude to those who care for us, then we are actually offering care to them. As long as we are alive and conscious, there will always be ways in which we can serve with a willing and joyful heart. Have you used all of your opportunities to do that for others?

75.
LEARN HOW TO WAIT.

And when they came together, he gave them this order: "Do not leave Jerusalem, but wait for the gift I told you about, the gift my Father promised. John baptized with water, but in a few days you will be baptized with the Holy Spirit."

Acts 1:4-5

Jesus had just risen from the dead, and although his apostles saw him, they were not quite ready to spread the good news of his resurrection. They knew that Jesus had been crucified, and they were afraid of what might happen to them. Who could blame them? Jesus knew their state of mind and that the time for them to preach the Good News had not yet come. And so he told them to wait. They were to wait for the Holy Spirit, whose energy would overcome their fears and empower them to do the task for which they had been chosen. The stakes were high. It was imperative for the people to hear the Good News. Their lives would be woefully incomplete if they did not hear it. And it was imperative for the apostles to spread the Good News. Their lives would be incomplete if they did not follow their calling. But in spite of this double urgency, they were told to wait.

Jesus himself was a master of waiting. He waited for thirty years before he gathered his apostles together and revealed his Father's message of Good News. Why so long a wait? And if the mission of the apostles was so urgent, why wasn't the Holy Spirit given to them right away? And then we can ask why it seems to take so long for us to understand and to live the message of Jesus. We don't have a full answer. All we know is that in this life, things take time. We pass through long months of winter before the new life of spring comes to revitalize us. And then it will take more months for spring's blossoms to ripen into flowers and fruit. And along with all of these processes, we too are growing.

Yet it takes years before we enjoy psychological and spiritual maturity. We might prefer things to be otherwise, but waiting seems to be as inevitable in our lives as snow is to winter.

Perhaps we can learn something from the experience of waiting. The experience shows us that we cannot always make things happen in our lives as quickly as we might wish. God will make things happen as they should when we are ready for what he wants to give us. For example, he touches us with his Spirit, but he waits for us while we grow in our capacity to accept what the Spirit gives. He calls us to forgive someone who has hurt us, but he waits while we get to the point where we are able to forgive. And in the process of forgiveness, we wait for others to reach the point where they can forgive us. In the midst of the waiting, we pray that God's Spirit may touch our lives and the lives of others with the power to change and grow. While doing what we can to help, we believe that God will eventually bring the best out of any situation, no matter what difficulties are involved. How he does that, well, that will be his problem. Our task is to do what we can while patiently waiting with trust for the fullness of what God will do. If we can do this, we will have peace of mind. Are you up to the task?

76.
LEARN TO LOVE SILENCE.

"But when you pray, go to your room, close the door, and pray to your Father, who is unseen."

Mt. 6:6

These words were directed to those who enjoyed praying publicly so that they could be seen by others. That may not be much of a problem in our culture, but because Scripture often has a significance that goes beyond its literal meaning, it can help us with problems we face today. Our problem is the multitude of TV and cell phone distractions that pulverize our minds into numbness. We are losing our ability to focus on things that should be meaningful and important to us. We need the silence that comes from going to our room and closing the door. How else will we able to hear God's inspirations within ourselves more fully and find peace of mind?

Going to your room and closing the door is a rejuvenating way of experiencing silence, reducing stress, and being attentive to God's presence. Closing the door can be seen as a metaphor for the need to shut out the distractions that keep us from focusing our minds. Jesus invites us to rest in his presence and to experience the peace that flows from spending quality time with him. For this, we need occasional periods of silence, time to close the door.

We may feel some resistance within ourselves when we start the practice of closing our door. All kinds of images might show up in our minds, and the thought comes up—here I am sitting when there are so many things that I have to do. But if you want to do all those things well, learn first to sit quietly. When asked why he took a one-month vacation every year, Oliver Wendell Holmes said that he took that time off because he could not accomplish in twelve months what he could do in eleven. A marvelous insight! The same principle works when we take quiet time on a daily basis. We work more efficiently throughout the day because we become more peaceful, less distracted, and more capable of focusing our thoughts. And so, resist the temptation to avoid closing your door. If you stick with setting aside a period of daily quiet time, you will see not only that the process will become easier, but also that it will become something you look forward to. You will be pleased with the fruit it will bear, and you will wonder how you ever lived your life without it.

Close your door, and sit in a comfortable position with your back straight and both feet on the floor. In order to help you relax, pay attention to the rhythm of your breathing for a few minutes. Breathe deeply from your abdomen, but without straining. Place your hand briefly on your abdomen, and if it rises as you breathe, then you are breathing correctly. Start with a very short reading from a spiritual book if you wish. All of this is a preparation for what follows and should not take more than several minutes.

The core of this prayerful exercise is simply to spend quiet time with God. You can begin by choosing a mantra and then repeating it prayerfully several times. An example of a mantra would be, "Lord Jesus Christ, Son of God, have mercy on me, a sinner." You can formulate your own mantra, but it should be very short. After you say it prayerfully once or twice, simply sit quietly with the Lord, and rest in the silence. If you become distracted, you can repeat your mantra once or twice to re-collect yourself, and then return immediately to the silence. Rest in the silence for as long as it is comfortable for you.

More information on this kind of prayer can be found in books that deal with centering prayer. The term "centering prayer" can also be looked up on the Internet. Spiritual directors could also be helpful with any questions that may arise with your prayer life. They can often be found in retreat houses and in parishes.

If we persevere with some form of quiet prayer, a greater sense of God's presence and guidance will take root within us. Ideally, all of our prayer should gradually lead us to a deeper silence, where thoughts fall away and we are simply left with the reality of God's presence. This is a wonderful antidote for the hectic pace of daily life and a good way to calm the stressful distractions of our minds. It is truly a pathway to joy that can affect your whole day! Are you ready to close the door?

77.

PAY DAILY ATTENTION TO WHERE YOU ARE GOING.

If one of you is planning to build a tower, he sits down first and figures out what it will cost, to see if he has enough money to finish the job. If he doesn't, he will not be able to finish the tower after laying the foundation; and all who see what happened will make fun of him.

Luke 14:28-29

Have you ever made a resolution to exercise, eat more healthfully, get more rest, and do all those things that would contribute to a healthier lifestyle? And then did you notice that, bit by bit, various parts of your resolution began to erode? You may have had no clear intention to shift into reverse gear, but perhaps you found yourself shaving off a half hour from your nightly rest, eating more junk food a little at a time, and shortening your planned time for exercise. And it all took place without your full realization of what was happening: an interesting comparison to what may have happened to the tower builder in Jesus' parable!

We sometimes fail in our decisions to live lives that are physically healthy, and similar failures can occur in our spiritual lives. We make a resolution to spend daily quiet time with God, and gradually the time spent begins to shorten. We make a resolution to feed our minds and hearts often with spiritual reading, but we spend less and less time on this nourishing help to prayer. And then one day we make a terrible discovery. We are hardly doing anything at all to expand the joys of our interior journey with God. How did we get that way? How did this happen? Well, we forgot to pay attention to where we were going.

Making a resolution to deepen your spiritual life is like Jesus' example of building a tower. You need to ask yourself if you've got the stuff to make it work. Are you really committed to build it? Do you have the faith to believe that Jesus will help you when the commitment becomes difficult? And will you take time daily to see if you are sabotaging yourself by shortening your time for reflection and prayer? The results of small infidelities accumulate gradually, and if you don't examine yourself, you may not be aware of what you are doing until a lot of damage has already been done. Then your spiritual edifice becomes like the tower that was never built. But there is no need for any of this to happen if you do one thing: pay attention every day to where you are going. This is an important part of self-knowledge. How important is it to you?

78.

REMEMBER THAT YOUR TIME ON EARTH IS SHORT.

What I mean, my brothers, is this: There is not much time left...For this world, as it is now, will not last much longer.

1 Cor. 7:29, 31.

This may not sound like good news, and it may not seem that a realization of time's shortness could lead you to joy. But if you realize that your time on earth is short, you will live your life to the fullest extent that you can in this present moment. You will live more deeply and dynamically, and that kind of an approach to life would offer you a greater sense of joy. Imagine that you knew you had only three months to live. How would that knowledge influence the choices you might make? Would there be a greater urgency to tell a loved one how important he or she is to you? Would there be a greater necessity to forgive someone who had hurt you? Is there something you have always wanted to do, but kept putting off? If these things are important to you, enjoy the satisfaction of doing them now. There may not be a tomorrow in which to do them.

This life is good when we live it fully and dynamically, but even though that is true, we realize that we can never be completely fulfilled during our lifetime on earth. The fullness of our joy will be experienced only when we resurrect to new life. And since this present life is short, that experience is closer than we might think. I know people who truly love this life, but who at the same time look forward eagerly to the fullness of joy in the resurrected life that Jesus promises to give when this life ends. They are like couples who enjoy their engagement period, but who are thankful that it is short, because they look forward to the full joy of the marriage relationship. In comparison, our life on earth is like the engagement period, and our life of resurrection will be like the marriage. Then we will experience the fullness of loving union with God, with one another, and with the entirety of God's creation.

Perhaps, then, reflecting on the shortness of this life might help us to live more fully during the time we have. And it might help us to appreciate the promise of the fuller life that is yet to come. Not everyone may view the shortness of this life in such a positive way, but such views are pathways that can lead to joy. Could these thoughts make sense to you?

79.

THINK BIG!

"I am telling you the truth: Whoever believes in me will do what I do—yes, he will do even greater things, because I am going to the Father."

John 14:12

Our accomplishments have their beginnings in our minds and hearts. It is there that these words of Jesus need to take root. When our faith allows his words to grow within ourselves, we discover a power that allows us to do what we thought could never be done. I am thinking of the power to forgive someone who hurt us deeply, someone we may have hated so much that the hatred almost became a part of our lives. I am thinking of the power to overcome an addiction that may have tied us in knots for more years than we might care to admit. And I am thinking of the power to overcome a fear so great that it kept us from doing courageously and honorably what we knew we should have done. Overcoming situations like these may seem like miracles to us, but that may be what Jesus had in mind when he said that we will do what he does—yes, even greater things. This is what faith in the power of Jesus can accomplish. We are encouraged to think big.

When I think of these words of Jesus, I am filled with gratitude, but then I wonder—is there a limit to what his power allows me to do? How do I know that all of the seemingly impossible things I want to do are in accord with his will? The answer seems to be that I would need to be aware of his will as much as I can, and this awareness can only grow through prayer. Everyone who spends time with God in prayer will come to know his guidance and inspiration. This is how we come to know the mind of God and to know what he wants to give us and what he wants us to do. There is a parallel here with our experiences of friendship. When we spend years of quality time with a friend, we come to know her heart and her mind. We know how to respond to her, and at the same time, we realize how our friend is likely to respond to our needs. So it is in our relationship with God.

In the biblical passage quoted above, Jesus promises that we will do what he does. That promise is bound up with the fact that he is going to the Father. The human nature of Jesus will pass beyond space and time into eternity, and so he will have the power to touch us in ways that go beyond what he could do before his resurrection. We rely on his intercession with the Father. We rely on his sending of the Holy Spirit. So of course, we will do what he does. And it follows, then, that we can think big. Does this promise of Jesus bring a greater sense of meaning to your life?

80.

ASK, ASK, AND NEVER STOP ASKING.

"In a certain town there was a judge who neither feared God nor respected man. And there was a widow in that same town who kept coming to him and pleading for her rights, saying, 'Help me against my opponent!' For a long time the judge refused to act, but at last he said to himself, 'Even though I don't fear God or respect man, yet because of all the trouble this widow is giving me, I will see to it that she gets her rights. If I don't, she will keep on coming and finally wear me out!'"

Luke 18:2-5

It would be hard to miss the point of Jesus' story. Perseverance is the key to successful prayer. One could ask, though, why we often have to wait so long for an answer. Why do we have to keep asking when God could give an answer anytime he wished? Or does God wait for the best time to answer? These are problems that seem to defy easy solutions. One thing seems clear, though. The need to ask is paramount in Jesus' teaching about prayer. I think this is because our incompleteness defines a good part of who we are, and that determines our continuing need for God. We are a reservoir of needs. No matter how altruistic we are, this is a part of the reason why we reach out to friends and extend our hands to God. The need to keep on asking will always serve as a reminder of who we are—people who have to depend on God for their survival and for their well-being.

We become more aware of our neediness and our dependence on God when God temporarily leaves us in our state of need. If every request were answered at once, it might seem to us that we were controlling God, as it were, or that somehow God existed to do our will, rather than the other way around. In conjunction with that, we would probably lose our sense of dependency that is an essential mark of a right relationship with God. So perhaps there is a pedagogical value in Jesus' teaching that we need to ask and never to stop asking for what we need.

No matter how mysterious God's ways seem, the gift of faith enables us to believe that God loves us tenderly, and that he will always bring the best out of any situation that confronts us. It seems to me that this gift of faith comes to those who have a deep prayer life. It is through prayer that we come to know that God loves us, that he is trustworthy, and that ultimately he will do what is best for us. And it is through prayer that we come to know what we should ask for and what those things are that cannot be given. Do you have the faith to believe that God will show you what you should ask for, and that he will give you the perseverance to keep asking for it?

81.

WHAT YOUR MOST PRECIOUS GIFT IS, AND HOW TO UNWRAP IT.

The Word became a human being and, full of grace and truth, lived among us.

John 1:14.

A man lived on a farm in a remote part of India. He wanted to visit a friend who lived several hundred miles away, but he had no car. The only means of transportation was a bus, and the trip was difficult for him due to his arthritic knees and back. His friend was on hand to meet him when the bus rolled into the station, and he noticed the pain on the man's face as he came out of the bus. His friend said, "When I saw the pain on your face as you arrived, I realized what you must have gone through in order to be here. Then I understood how important our friendship is to you."

If you really love someone, you want to be with him or her. And you will do anything to keep in touch. That's a sign of your love. We understand this instinctively, and it is our way of knowing that we are loved. When we apply this understanding to our relationship with God, we see more clearly why God sent his Son to live in our midst. God's love for us means that he wanted to be present to us, because that is the hallmark of all love and friendship. And he wanted us to know how much we are loved.

God's presence is always with us, of course, and that means that his guidance and inspiration continually touch our lives. But even though this is true, we long for a more concrete sign of God's presence, just as we long for concrete signs from those who love us. If there are no signs, we tend to doubt the love. And so God gave us a concrete sign. He sent Jesus. Jesus is God's supreme gift, a gift of God's presence, but we never experience this deeply in our hearts unless we unwrap the gift. Unwrapping God's gift and appreciating it is our gift to God. The unwrapping takes place when we prayerfully reflect on the meaning of the gift. I think it is only through prayerful reflection that we come to a fuller understanding of Jesus as the gift of God's presence that reveals how deeply we are loved. If we do not savor the gift, we miss its full significance. It remains hidden under the wrappings.

What does a friend most want from us? To appreciate her presence and her love! What does God want from us? The same thing!

Our most precious gift is Jesus, who reveals the love of God, a love so strong that it insists on being with us always. That's what we discover when we unwrap the gift through prayerful reflection. What a wonderful pathway to joy. Have you taken the time to unwrap the gift?

82.

OUR BLESSINGS ARE BEYOND MEASURE.

"As for you, how fortunate you are! Your eyes see and your ears hear. I assure you that many prophets and many of God's people wanted very much to see what you see, but they could not, and to hear what you hear, but they did not."

Mt. 13:16-17

I think most people have a deep longing to know that their lives have meaning and that a benevolent God cares for them each day of their lives. Various philosophical systems and religions have tried to address this need, and it is possible to learn valuable lessons from them. But Jesus addressed this need in a unique way. He told us that we are unconditionally loved by God, and that he was God's Son, sent by the Father to save us through his passion, death, and resurrection. He told us further that his loving power would be with us always, helping us where we have need, and that death was not the end of our lives. He promised a resurrection into new life, where death would no longer have any hold over us, and our resurrected lives would be bound up with his life forever. Ineffable, everlasting union with God and with all those we loved on earth! Here was a message people longed to hear. We have seen and heard what others have longed to see and hear. Indeed, we are fortunate and our blessings are beyond measure. How different our lives would have been if we had never heard the message of Jesus.

Our blessings are beyond measure, but we only come to see this when we reflect on what our blessings are. Think of the blessings of the Eucharist, the presence of Jesus, who comes to us in the sacramental sign of a meal. We can receive his presence each day if we wish, but there are others who have not even heard that there is such a thing as the Eucharist. Think of the blessings of God's forgiveness. God reveals himself as a compassionate God, one who does not hold our sins against us. Wherever there is true turning away from sin, there is God's forgiveness with its gift of peace. These are all a part of God's revelation, which we have heard. No wonder that Jesus called us "fortunate." When we think about our good fortune and what it means to us, then we desire that others might share in what we are enjoying. Our prayer should be that others will also have an opportunity to hear this revelation, that they may know the blessings that we have known.

How have Jesus' words been a blessing to you?

83.

BE CONTENT WITH WHAT YOU ARE ABLE TO DO.

Some tax collectors came to be baptized, and they asked him, "Teacher, what are we to do?"

"Don't collect more than is legal," he told them.

Some soldiers also asked him, "What about us? What are we to do?"

He said to them, "Don't take money from anyone by force or accuse anyone falsely. Be content with your pay."

Luke 3:12-14

These words invite us to see the value in the ordinary realities of our lives. The soldiers and tax collectors are not told to do something other than what they are doing. But they are told to act honestly and justly in what they do. The pathway to a joy-filled existence can be found through the activities that we do every day. If we have found a career that fits us and we do our work well, we are on a good path. If we are faithful to our obligations, we walk in a way that brings peace to others and to ourselves. Perhaps the challenge is to see the value in what we do each day and to be thankful for what we have been able to accomplish through the power of God working within us.

When we look back on our lives, we may not discover anything extraordinary in what we have done. But the lives of those we love would have been poorer if we had not been a part of them. The same is true in reverse. Our lives would have been poorer if those we love had not been a part of us. Love given and love received have made us to be who we are, and all of this has taken place in the everyday circumstances of our lives. Such is the value of all the ordinary things we do for others. What a great reason for being joyful about our lives!

We miss the meaning of our lives when we are unaware of all the ordinary things that God has enabled us to do. The following story reflects this idea. A woman who was dying asked me if I thought she would go to heaven. The question took me by surprise, and I reminded her of all that she had done for her community, and all the people who had benefited from her work and her friendship. She seemed genuinely surprised that her life had shown so much value. There is a problem when we do not appreciate the good that God has allowed us to accomplish, because then we miss the value and meaning of what we have done.

Are you able to see the value and meaning of what you have done, and to be grateful for it? Are you content with what God has enabled you to do?

84.

GOD RESCUES US WHEN WE
CANNOT HELP OURSELVES.

The Egyptians treated us harshly and forced us to work as slaves. Then we cried out for help to the Lord, the God of our ancestors. He heard us and saw our suffering, hardship, and misery .By his great power and strength he rescued us from Egypt. He worked miracles and wonders, and caused terrifying things to happen. He brought us here and gave us this rich and fertile land.

Deut. 26:6-9

We can read this story of redemption merely as a historical account of what God did for the Hebrews thousands of years ago. In that case, it might be an interesting story, but it would probably have little meaning for our everyday lives. Suppose, though, that we were to read these words as words that God is addressing to us in our circumstances in this present moment. The words would have a far greater impact, because they would have a personal meaning for us. Just as the Hebrews were stuck in a situation of hardship and slavery with no apparent way out, so we sometimes seem stuck in untenable situations with little hope of relief. And so we call out for rescue. What kind of attitude should be entwined with our plea, and how might we experience God's response?

We might get some answers to those questions by putting ourselves into this Biblical story of redemption. This can be a helpful spiritual exercise, and it will take only a few minutes of your time. Imagine being with these ancient Hebrews, oppressed, forced into a lifestyle that is degrading, and without any quick prospects for change. Every day you are compelled to do work that is relentlessly hard, has no benefit to you, and gives no sense of meaning in your life. You are not respected or appreciated, and you are ill-treated by those who oppress you. And this goes on day after day. You call out to God in faith, but your faith has to be thoroughly leavened with patience, because it appears that there will be no immediate answer to your plea. You cannot free yourself from this difficult situation. You can only wait patiently for the circumstances to develop that will finally enable you to be set free. And that patience will not be something that you can achieve by yourself. Patience will be God's gift to you. The ability to wait with trust for deliverance is beyond your abilities, but God makes it possible within you. God did deliver the ancient Hebrews from their oppression. He will also deliver you from yours.

In our day, we are not oppressed in the way the ancient Hebrews were. Our oppression may come from within ourselves in the form of painful attitudes and habits that are hard to change. Or perhaps we are stuck with a form of work that brings no satisfaction. Sometimes we find ourselves in relationships that are oppressive and we don't know how to change them. And then there will be times when our bodies oppress us with sickness. In all of these situations, we cry out to the Lord. We believe that he hears us because he loves us, but for reasons we do not understand, the response takes time, or perhaps it comes in ways we do not expect. And so, just as the ancient Hebrews did, we come before the Lord with trust and with patience, while doing what we can to ease our difficulties.

We live without always understanding why things happen as they do. But we know in faith that ultimately God will bring deliverance where we need it. When you feel oppressed, do you remember to ask God for the faith, patience, and insight that will help you through your trials?

85.

IF YOU WANT THE GLORY, YOU HAVE TO PAY THE PRICE.

"When you sit on your throne in your glorious Kingdom, we want you to let us sit with you, one at your right and one at your left."

Jesus said to them, "You don't know what you are asking for. Can you drink the cup of suffering that I must drink? Can you be baptized in the way I must be baptized?"

Mark 10:37-38

Everything valuable has its price. The two apostles asking Jesus for privileged positions in his Kingdom are warned about the cost in suffering that would have to be paid. All of the apostles, with the exception of John, died as martyrs for the sake of the gospel. Suffering of some kind is the coin that has to be paid for any worthwhile goal in life. This may not seem like joyful news, but our willing acceptance of it puts us on a pathway that ultimately leads to joy. If we travel our path with fidelity, accepting both its joys and its sufferings, we reach the intended goal that we have chosen. At that point, the price we paid is eclipsed by the experience of joy. Jesus told us, *"When a woman is about to give birth, she is sad because her hour of suffering has come; but when the baby is born, she forgets her suffering, because she is happy that a baby has been born into the world." John 16:21*

The death of our self-centeredness is the price we pay for living in the Kingdom in union with Jesus. Putting to death all of our attitudes that are at war with the good news of Jesus is a painful process, a kind of death that we would naturally like to avoid. Yet, there is no other way to the Kingdom, and to the experience of full, loving union with God.

This is the cross Jesus requires all of his followers to carry. I think this becomes meaningful to us to the extent that we identify the particular crosses Jesus asks us to carry. Then we discover where we have to die in order to live. What anger, fear, lust, laziness, wasting of time, or refusal to love do we have to put to death within ourselves? How do those freely chosen states of mind keep us out of the Kingdom? And then perhaps we come to see how difficult it is to give them up. At that point, we discover the price we have to pay.

We have to be careful, though, about how we interpret the phrase "paying the price." We can never buy our way into the Kingdom. Citizenship in the Kingdom is given freely by God. We cannot earn it. We can only accept it. Paying the price, then, would mean dying to the obstacles within ourselves that make it difficult or even impossible for us to accept God's free gift. Dying to those obstacles is where we encounter the cross, and it is only with God's freely given power that we are able to carry it. He is the one who sets us free, but not without our cooperation. Are you willing to pay the price?

86.

DIVINE EXPECTATIONS BRING DIVINE REWARDS.

"Suppose one of you has a servant who is plowing or looking after the sheep. When he comes in from the field, do you tell him to hurry along and eat his meal? Of course not! Instead you say to him, 'Get my supper ready, then put on your apron and wait on me while I eat and drink; after that you may have your meal.' The servant does not deserve thanks for obeying orders, does he? It is the same for you; when you have done all that you have been told to do, say, 'We are ordinary servants; we have only done our duty.'"

Luke 17:7-11

"How happy are those servants whose master finds them awake and ready when he returns! I tell you, he will take off his coat, have them sit down, and will wait on them."

Luke 12:37

I have sometimes wondered at the paradox that jumps out at me whenever I compare these two texts. The first text tells me that God has expectations of me, and that it is my duty to fulfill them. He is the Master, the one in charge, and my job is to live in accordance with his word. He has set down the parameters in which my life is to be lived, and if I want things to work out, I have to live within those parameters. That is the way things are, and I should expect no reward for doing what needs to be done. Who would expect to be rewarded in a special way for following traffic laws or paying one's income tax? From this point of view, the text makes perfect sense, and one would be foolish not to follow it. But if you were to isolate this text from the rest of the gospel, it would give a very uninviting picture of God. It portrays our relationship with God as one of duty, and quite honestly, that does not seem very enticing. Fortunately, there is much more to the relationship, as the second text shows.

When you read the second text, you again find servants who are simply fulfilling expectations, just doing what they are supposed to do. Here, though, the emphasis is not on duty, but rather on the appreciation the master has for the fidelity of his servants. If you make the message personal, it tells you that God appreciates what you do for him and for others. That gives you a new understanding of the importance of what you do, and of the love that God has for you. There is nothing hard to understand here, because when you love someone, you notice all the good that person does for you, no matter how small the deed. The more you love, the more you will notice! So of course God will notice and appreciate all the good that you do, because that is the sign of one who loves.

There is an expectation that we as creatures should do the will of the one who gave us life. We become aware of the expectation through God's word and the inspiration that he puts into our hearts through the working of the Holy Spirit. It is our duty to respond even if no reward were to be given. And yet God is so generous that our obedient responses are rewarded with an ever-increasing share in his life. Just by being faithful and dutiful servants, we are invited into the intimacy of the Master's table. Servants do not usually get that kind of treatment, but ultimately, we are not treated as servants. Are you aware of the generosity of God's love for you?

87.

FROM OUR BARRENNESS, GOD
BRINGS FORTH LIFE.

*"Don't be afraid, Zechariah! God has heard your prayer,
and your wife Elizabeth will bear you a son."*

Luke 1:13

The first chapter of Luke tells us that both Elizabeth and Zechariah were old, and that Elizabeth was unable to bear children. Yet in the midst of these seemingly impossible circumstances, Elizabeth gave birth to John the Baptist. The story brings back memories of Abraham and Sarah, who were unable to have children until Sarah, in her old age, became the mother of Isaac. It must have seemed to these women as they entered old age that the experience of motherhood laid far beyond the horizon of their wildest dreams. And yet, from their barrenness, God brought forth life, and their children influenced the destinies of untold numbers of people. These stories show how God brought life in unexpected ways. Does he still do that today?

These stories would have a far greater impact on us if we could see how they might apply to what happens in the circumstances of our own lives. To make these stories personally relevant, you could ask where you experience a kind of barrenness in your life. You might experience the barrenness as a sense of dullness, a lack of vitality, or a loss of meaning that would prompt you to pray for relief. These negative experiences could affect your spiritual life, your career, and even your friendships. You could ask God for a renewed sense of being alive and for a fruitfulness in your heart and mind that would bring you new energy and a new ability to love and serve others.

Zechariah and Elizabeth prayed for a long time before their prayer for fruitfulness was answered. Part of the mystery of life is why the waiting period sometimes seems so long. Maybe the answer is that we have to wait until we are ready to receive what we are praying for. For reasons we cannot understand, perhaps her old age was the best time for Elizabeth to become fruitful and bear her son John. Certainly this circumstance more clearly revealed the power of God working in her life, and it offered yet another proof that God accomplishes within us what we cannot do by ourselves. Were there also other reasons? We cannot know. We can only live with faith and trust in the way God answers our prayers.

The answer to our prayers for fruitfulness and vitality may come as a surprise, at a time when we are not expecting anything new. This seems to be what happened in the story of Elizabeth and Zechariah. For us, the surprise may come in the form of new friendships, new opportunities in our careers, or the discovery of forms of spirituality that bring new life in our relationship with God. These are all gifts that can bring greater vitality and fruitfulness to our prayer life, and to our relationships with others.

We all go through periods of life when a sense of barrenness seems to settle over us. Sometimes those periods are times of incubation, preparing us for something new. In any case, these are circumstances that we can bring to God in prayer, trusting that his answer will come in the way and in the time that is best. Do you believe that, from your barrenness, God will eventually bring forth life?

88.

FINDING IMPORTANCE IN THE SMALL THINGS THAT MAKE UP OUR LIVES.

"Whoever is faithful in small matters will be faithful in large ones; whoever is dishonest in small matters will be dishonest in large ones."

Luke 16:10

A piece of music is made up of many small notes. Even though they are small, each note is important. If you were to take any of them out, the music would not be as the composer meant it to be. Of course it is also possible to put wrong notes into a piece of music. This happens occasionally when I play the piano. Again, the music turns out not to be as the composer meant it to be.

The small acts of fidelity and kindness that we do for others are like the notes in a piece of music. Our good actions, no matter how small, make us to be as God meant us to be. That's why Jesus tells us that the small things we do are important, not only for others, but also for ourselves. This is a consoling thought to me, because much of what I do is not great or heroic, and because it is simply ordinary, it may sometimes go unnoticed. And yet these small actions are important, because without them, my life and the lives of others would be diminished.

It has always amazed me how pleased people are when you show them even a small amount of recognition. This is a good example of how a seemingly small thing can have importance for others. Sometimes my reminiscences bring back thoughts about the many small acts of love I have received from my parents over the span of so many years. If they were still alive, they might not remember them, and yet those acts enriched my life and made me to be who I am. From their place in heaven, though, I think my parents remember them, for their acts made them to be who they are, and in the fully conscious state that they now enjoy, that knowledge will be with them forever. A part of the joy of our resurrected life will be to recognize the value of the small acts of love and kindness that we have given and received. And then we will see that all of our small acts of love prepared us for the final great act of love, the final choice for God we are all called to make as we leave this life for our true home in heaven. Having been faithful in small matters, we will be faithful in large ones.

It would seem, then, that our awareness of the importance of the small things in our lives is a part of our pathway to joy, a part that we should treasure. Would you have thought that all of your small acts could have such value?

89.

LIVING WHERE WE ARE MEANT TO BE.

We, however, are citizens of heaven, and we eagerly wait for
our Savior, the Lord Jesus Christ, to come from heaven.

Phil. 3:20

We are only truly at home when we live in the heart of Jesus. If we live there, we are in some sense already in heaven, for we come to know his thoughts and his love. When we let Jesus' thoughts and love take over our lives, then we are saved from our sinfulness and incompleteness. We become one with him, and that lifts us up beyond ourselves to his level, where we find the true meaning of who we are meant to be.

We can only live in the heart of Jesus because he makes this possible for us. We can do nothing without him. But he will give us this gift if we ask with perseverance, because God's desire is that we should live in his heart. The gospel is clear on this point, because God gave the gospel as a revelation of the loving relationship he desires to have with us. We never could have figured this out by ourselves. But once it is revealed, God's loving attitude toward us should not be too hard to understand. We have strong desires to experience union with those we love. Should it be any different with God, whose very essence is love?

The revelation that we are citizens of heaven is meant to fill us with joy. But there is a problem. In the midst of a life filled with distractions, we forget where our true home is. And we may have to admit with some embarrassment that living in the heart of Jesus is at times not a priority for us. If that is the case, we miss out on the joy that intimacy with God is able to give us. There is a remedy, though, one that I have learned from others, and one that I have found to be useful for myself. Throughout the day I repeat a short prayer: "Lord, help me to love you." Frequent repetition of this prayer reminds me of the relationship with God that I want to have, and it keeps me open to the intimacy that God wants to give. You can use your own words if you wish, and the words you choose will slowly have an effect on your thoughts if you persevere with your prayer. There are, of course, different ways to pray, and this method is only one of many. But you might want to see if this works for you. If it does, you will have found another pathway that can bring you joy.

Do you realize that, even in the midst of your life on earth, you are at this moment a citizen of heaven?

90.

LEARNING FROM THE GOODNESS OF OTHERS.

Pay attention to those who follow the right example we have set for you.

Phil. 3:17

Is the world getting better or is it getting worse? Perhaps it depends on whom you pay attention to. If you read or listen to what the news media put in front of you, it might seem that the world is getting worse. But if you pay attention to the many people who live their lives with love and who genuinely care for others, then perhaps the world is not as bad as some might think. We can learn from such people, for they show us what our own lives can be like.

Recently an employee in an acute care center told me that she lost her temper due to an assignment that she received from her supervisor. Her demeanor and language caused her supervisor to take her to the administrator's office, where she gave a repeat performance of her anger. The administrator said, "You know, I could fire you right now for insubordination, but I don't want to do that. Mary [not her real name], why don't you just go back to work?" His kindness completely surprised her, and, somewhat in a daze, she went back to work. She is still working and has become quite happy with her job, as well as with her life in general.

After she told me this story, I thought deeply about the quality of the administrator's response, and two things occurred to me. First, it seemed to me that his attitude was a reflection of the way Jesus would have reacted toward this employee. And in fact, it is the way that Jesus consistently acts toward us as he forgives us when our behaviors miss the mark. Secondly, I saw his response as a model of the way I should act when others behave inappropriately toward me. Hearing this story and reflecting on it brought me a sense of joy, a feeling that most of us have when we come face to face with goodness.

This story is not the only one that has touched me with goodness recently. There have been many others, especially stories of people who remain cheerful caregivers even when they sometimes carry heavy burdens of their own. I have been privileged to witness many examples of this kind of self-forgetfulness. And there are so many other examples of goodness in other places and circumstances that I have witnessed. They have affected my life and they have brought me joy.

There is only one requirement for this to work in your life. You have to notice these examples. They are all around you, and it would be a great loss to you if you were to miss them. When you do notice them, then you can reflect on their beauty and see how they can be models for your own life. Do you take the time to notice the goodness of others and to learn from what you see?

91.

IF YOU LOVE, WHAT YOU DO IS NEVER IN VAIN.

We are honored and disgraced; we are insulted and praised. We are treated as liars, yet we speak the truth; as unknown, yet we are known by all; as though we were dead, but, as you see, we live on.

2 Cor. 6:8-9

St. Paul looked at his life, and as the above text shows, he experienced his efforts as a mixture of successes and failures. This could well be the story of our lives. We look at what we have tried to accomplish, and while we are thankful for what has worked out well, we may wonder why certain things did not. We may never know the answers, but it is important to believe that nothing we do is ever in vain, and that includes our failures. Success is not the most important value in our lives, and we do not always have control over the successful outcomes of what we do. The most important value is to do our best while acting with love, and there is where we have the control.

Imagine a situation in which parents love their children and teach them Christian values, but one of the children refuses those values and embraces a destructive lifestyle. And no matter what the parents say or do, the destructive lifestyle persists. A similar situation can happen in a classroom where a teacher, in spite of her best efforts, is unable to motivate a student. Or a person may try to reconcile with someone he has hurt, and find that his efforts are refused. Success can elude us in some of our personal relationships, and we can fail in our careers, but if we have done our best and acted with love, we did not act in vain. How can this be?

Every loving action we do has a positive effect on us, and because of that, our actions can have positive effects on all those who come in contact with us. That remains true even when we direct loving actions towards those who refuse to respond to us. So long as we avoid anger toward those persons, the love we have given to them will affect our personalities for the good. The love, then, will not have been given in vain. It will change us and it will shine through us in our contacts with others. But there seems to be something more. Not only our expressed actions, but even our unexpressed thoughts have effects on those around us, as the following example shows.

A scientist used a measuring device to discover how a plant reacted when its leaves were burned by a candle. The measuring device registered a response from the plant even before its leaves were singed. The plant could somehow "read" the scientist's negative response toward it. I think that in similar ways people sense our attitudes toward them, even before they are fully expressed. Loving personalities give off positive vibrations that affect others, and of course, the opposite is also true. We experience this phenomenon sometimes when walking into a room full of people whom we may not even know. We can sense the mood or the vibrations created by the group. We can also sense this in our one-on-one contacts with others.

Our good thoughts and actions affect both others and ourselves, and because of that, no good thought or action we do is ever done in vain. A particular person we want to help may refuse our offer, but the love we have given will always have a value, even if that person never changes. The love we gave will have changed us, and all those whose lives we touch will have benefited.

You may be saddened by people's refusal to accept your love, but the giving of that love is never in vain. All acts of love enrich you. Can you see how this works in your life?

92.

GOD CONTINUALLY RESHAPES OUR LIVES TO MAKE THEM MORE BEAUTIFUL.

The Lord said to me, "Go down to the potter's house, where I will give you my message." So I went there and saw the potter working at his wheel. Whenever a piece of pottery turned out imperfect, he would take the clay and make it into something else.

Jeremiah 18:1-5

Notice that even though the clay's form is changed, the clay itself is never discarded. This image of the potter refashioning his clay is an apt metaphor for what happens in our lives. Our existence is never discarded, but God does give it different shapes and forms that change over time. Sometimes the shapes of our lives change through God's inspirations that invite us to let our lives take on new forms. At other times, God uses the processes of nature to mold us into new forms as we pass through the stages of life from childhood to old age. And then sometimes our relationships with others become the arena in which God's grace forms us into new ways of being. In all of these situations, the clay of our lives is being molded into ever-new ways of expressing itself.

When I was a teenager, I felt a strong inspiration to enter a contemplative monastic community. This was an inspiration that gave a new form to my life, a new direction that has influenced me even to the present day. After sixteen years in that community, another inspiration came that pulled me toward a community that was more actively engaged in the apostolate. This move molded my spirituality in yet another way. The divine Potter was at work creating something new. He does this in the lives of each one of us.

I remember reading about a successful businessman who felt inspired to give up a high-paying position in his company and to return to school in order to earn a degree in psychology. He thought that he would be more helpful to others as a psychologist, and this choice resulted in a remolding of his life that brought him a new sense of purpose.

There are many examples of people being inspired to do something different with their lives, but not all inspirations necessarily propel them toward a radical remolding. Sometimes inspirations may come as an impulse to donate a few hours of time to a charitable cause. That may seem like a small thing, but a response to that impulse allows the divine Potter to mold their lives in ways that could not be done if they had been less generous.

God continues to mold us into new forms as he guides us in our growth from childhood, through adolescence and adulthood, and finally into old age. We are gradually fashioned through each stage into the fullness of what we are meant to be. Each time of life is important, for each new stage builds upon the previous one to bring us into greater maturity. The clay's substance remains the same, but at each stage of life, it is formed into something new. Ideally, our lives progress in wisdom and goodness as we evolve toward old age, and so old age should be treasured, rather than regretted, as sometimes happens in our society. If we have grown old well, with wisdom and grace, the final form of our clay should indeed be beautiful, more beautiful at its end than it was at its beginning. Perhaps you can see some of this process at work in your own life by comparing the wisdom you have now with what you had five or ten years ago.

Touched by inspirations and molded by our natural growth, we are constantly being reshaped. But the divine Potter is also at work in our lives through the influences of people who have touched our lives in significant ways. I owe much to the individuals whose love and insights have given new form and direction to my life. Truly, they have helped to mold me into what I am today, and I regard their presence in my life as a clear sign of the divine Potter's providential care and guidance. Our lives are deeply enriched when we become aware of those who influenced our lives for the good. We owe them a debt of gratitude that can never adequately be repaid. It is a great joy to reflect on our lives and to remember these people and what they have done for us.

We have been touched in many beautiful ways by the forming hands of God. Are you aware of the ways in which the divine Potter has been at work in your life?

93.

HAVE YOU SEEN THE LIGHT?

"The people who live in darkness will see a great light. On those who live in the dark land of death the light will shine."

Matthew 4:16

On the night before he died, Jesus washed his disciples' feet. This was an unenviable task usually performed by servants. Here we see God acting as a servant for us, to show how tenderly he regarded us, and to be a model for us to follow in our relationships with others. Then Jesus called us his friends, because he had told us everything that he had received from his Father. His message was meant to bring us joy. Of course, we could not live that message by our own strength alone, and so he promised that he would be with us always. He loved us even on the cross, dying there as a result of the rejection of those who would not accept him. And then, true to his promise, he rose to a new form of life that he invited us to share with him.

As beautiful as this is, one can know all these things and still not be in the light. It seems to me that one can be fully in the light only when he can apply all of these truths to himself in a way that totally engages his mind and heart. When one feels deeply in his mind and heart that God actually serves him every day through his help and inspirations, then he is in the light. When one believes that Jesus personally calls him his friend, and that Jesus is present to him intimately each day with his love and help, then he is in the light. When one believes that Jesus would have died for him alone, and that the invitation to follow him into resurrected life is a personal call to unimaginable intimacy, then he is in the light.

If we allow Jesus to be the absolute center of our lives and to transform us by his presence, then can we say that we have seen the light. If we have not made all of this personally meaningful, we have not seen much of anything. It all remains abstract. Ask yourself how deeply Jesus' words and Jesus' love have touched you in your daily life. Have you seen the light?

94.

FAITH IS NOT STATIC. IT IS MEANT TO GROW.

"I have much more to tell you, but now it would be too much for you to bear. When, however, the Spirit comes, who reveals the truth about God, he will lead you into all the truth."

John 16:12-13

When you love someone, you are never satisfied until you know as much about your beloved as the strength of your curiosity allows. That is the dynamic quality of love. It always wants to know and to experience as much as it can. And the growth in knowledge and experience of the one you love brings an ever-increasing joy and meaning to your life. It would be inconceivable that you would want this growth process to stop.

Something similar happens when people become interested in an activity that captivates their attention. A friend of mine developed an interest in sailing. One Sunday afternoon I went to his home for a visit and found his living room floor covered with strands of rope. The ropes were tied together with all the varieties of nautical knots that his research enabled him to find. I never understood why this accomplishment was so fulfilling for him, but then I never experienced his insatiable love for sailing. And it was that love that drove him to find out as much as he could about every aspect of his hobby.

It would be a great gift if that same dynamic were alive in our journey of faith. Our faith and our knowledge of God are meant to grow, just as our knowledge of those we love continues to grow. Jesus said that he had much more to tell his apostles, but that they were not ready to grasp all that he had to say. The same would be true for us. At any given moment of our lives, we can only grasp a certain amount of faith's meaning. But with the guidance of the Holy Spirit, our knowledge and understanding is meant to grow. That only happens if we are sufficiently interested to receive what the Spirit wishes to give.

People in love spend time together, paying attention to one another's gestures and words. My friend, in his love for sailing, learned to tie all kinds of nautical knots. Those who want to deepen their faith will spend time in prayer and meditate on the beauty of what God has revealed through his presence and his word. And they will nourish their meditation with books that can deepen their understanding of all that God reveals to them. One who does these things opens himself up to the guidance of the Holy Spirit, who helps him to penetrate more deeply into the mystery of God's presence and love. His faith will grow as God wills, and it will open up to him a pathway that leads to joy. Is your faith growing, and does that growth lead you to experience your life with greater meaning and joy?

95.

ALLOWING JESUS TO RESTORE OUR LIVES.

Then he walked over and touched the coffin, and the men carrying it stopped. Jesus said, "Young man! Get up I tell you!" The dead man sat up and began to talk, and Jesus gave him back to his mother.

Luke 7:14-15

The touch of Jesus restores life where there is death. One should expect this from Jesus, who is life itself. And his promise is that the divine touch will restore life to us when our lives on earth come to an end. But should we have to wait until then to experience the life-giving touch of God? Can those parts of us that are dead in this present moment be brought back to life by Jesus' healing touch?

Perhaps many of us go through our daily lives without realizing how deeply we are loved. We receive approbation and affection, and fail to recognize the beauty of the gift that is given to us. This has happened to me more than once, and it may be more common in our lives than we would care to admit. If nothing registers when people give us the gift of their love, then we are dead to the life-giving experience that their love is meant to give. It seems important to know if we are missing out here, because if we are, something beautiful in our lives will be lost to us. If we examine ourselves and become aware of this deadness, we can ask Jesus to bring us back to life. We can ask for the insight to become alive to the love that is given us, and to appreciate what we receive.

The tragedy of deadness can touch many areas of our existence in which we are meant to be alive. Probably millions of people go through significant parts of their lives failing to notice God's creative presence in the beauty of nature that surrounds them. The stars, sunlight, trees, flowers, and brooks all shine out to us with the radiance of God's goodness. Our lives are enriched when we pay attention to these blessings. When was the last time you noticed the beauty that overflows from God's creation? If the beauty of nature fails to refresh you and renew your life, then you can ask Jesus to help you come alive in this area of your life where you are dead.

Are we dead sometimes to the sufferings of others? Millions of children go to bed hungry every night, and incredibly, some of them are here even in our own country. Imagine how it might feel to end the day with an empty stomach, and with the pangs of hunger that would rob you of a restful night of sleep. But there is a remedy. We can support the worthwhile agencies that alleviate the horror of hunger. Compassionate people are not satisfied unless they help to reduce the sufferings of others. And by doing that, they find joy in their own lives. People who need us are always in our midst. Are we dead to their plight?

Perhaps we could reflect on our lives to discover those parts of us where we are dead. Are you willing to ask for Jesus' healing touch where you need it, so that you can be brought back to life?

96.

FINDING GOD'S PRESENCE IN THE EUCHARISTIC COMMUNITY.

"For where two or three come together in my name, I am there with them."

Mt. 18:20

An experience of prayer shared together is one of the deepest experiences of community. When there is a common contemplation and reception of the Lord's gifts, our fellowship is lifted up to its highest level. Here we share not only our own gifts, but divine gifts. This is why participation in Eucharistic celebrations is so important. Sharing in merely social celebrations, as necessary and beautiful as they sometimes can be, is not enough to bring us to the depths of sharing that God wants us to experience with one another.

When we take our place in celebrations of the Eucharist, we are all fed from the same source. We are receivers of God's word, and we receive his very presence in the consecrated bread and wine, which become the divine food sustaining our lives. It is a beautiful experience for me when I realize that the same divine life that animates me, animates all of us and makes us one. Our union with one another finds its perfect fulfillment in our sharing together in this life of God. We are one in Jesus Christ. This is the faith experience that brings much joy when we participate in the celebration of the Eucharist with an awareness of its meaning. The point is to stay awake to the meaning of what is happening in the celebration.

We all hear the same words of the gospel, but our experience of those words may differ according to what we find most important for our own lives. Since our experiences differ, we can learn much from sharing our insights as to the gospel's meaning for us. People have told me that they discuss the gospel and homily on their way home from church. What a wonderful way for members of a family to share their insights about what is important to them. I think this is a fruitful source of joy and also a beautiful way to increase the experience of family love and solidarity.

Participation in celebrations of worship not only strengthens our faith, but also helps us to strengthen the faith of others. Simply by showing up and being attentive, we demonstrate to others the importance of the Eucharist for us, and in that way, we can have a positive influence on others. And it works the other way around too. When we see the faith of others, they can have a positive influence on us. This has often happened to me when I celebrate the Eucharist. As I look at the people gathered there and see their interest and their attention, I am strengthened in my faith. Here you have one of the many blessings of a Eucharistic community.

We cannot experience this kind of reinforcing joy without others, who make it possible for us. Imagine celebrating the Fourth of July by yourself, just you carrying the flag alone down the street with no band, no onlookers to share the celebration or the values it signifies. Or a Christmas celebration where you sit alone, opening gifts that you bought for yourself. This would seem ridiculous to us. We need a community to celebrate. Without community, an essential experience is missing from our lives. And how true this is for our spiritual need to celebrate our common friendship with God in communion with one another. It gives an outward expression to the love that we feel in our hearts, while enabling us to be strengthened by the faith of others. Look for a community where you can find this experience. Can you see this as a life-giving pathway that nourishes you on your way to God?

97.
FORMING YOUR LEGACY.

So Eleazar died. But his courageous death was remembered
as a glorious example, not only by young people, but by
the entire nation as well.

2 Maccabees 6:31

When you die, how will you be remembered? How will your life have touched and enriched others? You can see the significance of these questions when you consider how your life has been influenced by others who were important to you, and how you have been formed by their presence in your life. They have helped you to become the person you are. You never see clearly how this works unless you reflect on the lives of those who have touched your own.

As I reflect on my parents' lives, their fidelity and self-forgetfulness present themselves to my mind. It would have been impossible for me not to be influenced by the way they lived. I can think of the many ways in which they showed their love, and they are all embedded in my memory.

Relatives and friends have also played their part in forming me to be who I am. I could give so many examples, but it is more important now for you to reflect on the legacies you have received in your life. Once you are aware of them, you can ask what kind of legacy you want to leave for others. The question contains a good deal of possibilities for joy, for you will discover that your life has already touched others in ways that have brought joy to them.

No human being ever leaves a perfect legacy, of course. We have all made mistakes, but we can learn from them, and that can show us how to improve the quality of the example we leave for others. Most of us will leave legacies that are permeated with goodness. It seems best to be more aware of the positive influences we will leave to others, and to be thankful to God, who makes those influences possible. All good choices we are making now are gifts of God to us, and through us, they will become gifts to others. And so it is important for us to form our legacy well, because that will be our gift to those we love. What kind of legacy will you leave to those you love?

98.

SEEING YOURSELF AS A TREASURED PLACE IN WHICH GOD DWELLS.

Don't you know that your body is the temple of the Holy Spirit, who lives in you and who was given to you by God? You do not belong to yourselves, but to God; he bought you for a price. So use your bodies for God's glory.

1 Cor. 6:19-20

Our bodily senses are our first revealers of God's presence in our lives. Our eyes and ears are the pathways over which the knowledge of God's word begins to make its home within us. No wonder, then, that the Holy Spirit makes a temple of our bodies. They are holy. Without them, it would have been impossible for us to know anything of God's intimate love.

Our bodies are holy not only because they reveal God's presence through our senses, although that in itself would be enough for us to have a reverence for them. But there is more. If our bodies are the Holy Spirit's temples, that means that his presence is within them. They are a part of who we are, and God loves us so much that there is no part of us that is unimportant to him. He is present to the totality of our being, and that is what gives our lives an orientation toward holiness. Our natural response is to respect all things that are related to what is holy. And so we respect our bodies as temples of the Holy Spirit, because he calls us to holiness by choosing to reside within us.

It follows that we will care appropriately for our bodies, not only to stay physically and morally healthy, but also as a sign of respect for what our bodies are: temples of the Holy Spirit. We belong to God because he continually sustains us with his loving presence. We can let that understanding determine how deeply we will respect our bodies made holy by God's presence within them. And this will open yet another pathway that will lead us to joy. Does the understanding of your body as the temple of the Holy Spirit bring you joy?

99.

OUR BURDENS ARE LIGHTENED WHEN WE BEAR THEM WITH LOVE.

"For the yoke I will give you is easy, and the load I will put on you is light."

Mt. 11:30

Years ago, I remember seeing a poster of a boy carrying a smaller boy on his shoulders, with a caption that read, "He ain't heavy, Father. He's my brother." That poster reminded me of what Jesus said about the yoke each one of us has to bear. The yoke he gives will be easy. I think we are able to perceive our yoke that way, but only when it is borne with love. Haven't we all experienced the truth of this?

One day as my mother was reminiscing about our early family life, she said to me, "You were always such a good boy. You even came out to the kitchen every night to help with the dishes without being asked." What I didn't tell her was that the whole experience was a drudgery for me. And the only reason I came out was because I knew I would eventually be in big trouble if I didn't show up. I was about eight years old at the time, and there wasn't enough love in me in those dish-wiping moments to make the burden light. Fortunately, most eight-year-olds eventually grow up.

An important pathway to God is through a compassionate caring for others, doing good to others who can benefit from our help. When we travel along this pathway, we do experience a joy, for then we are imitating God who constantly cares for us. And when we willingly do what God does, we realize the deepest meaning of who we are meant to be. If we miss this, our yoke becomes a heavy burden, and we miss our opportunity for joy. This is obvious to me as I watch health care staff caring for those who are elderly and sick. At times, all caregivers become tired or stressed. But when they have a love for their patients, they usually show a gentleness and cheerfulness that distinguishes them from those who feel little affection toward those they serve. Love makes the yoke seem easier, and love gives the energy to do what needs to be done.

The same principle is true outside of health care too, of course. The principle is at work as we serve one another in our families, as we relate to our friends, and as we relate to those in our work place. The needs of people will sometimes seem like a yoke that falls upon us, but the yoke will be easier in proportion to the amount of love we bring to it. Have you noticed that this is true in your life?

100.
CHOOSE LIFE!

I am now giving you the choice between life and death, between God's blessing and God's curse, and I call heaven and earth to witness the choice you make. Choose life.

Deut. 30:19

The one who gazes into God's open heart, and takes what he finds there into his own heart, is the one who chooses life. God's revelation shows us how the meaning of life can be found and experienced. One who receives God's word discovers God's presence within himself, and receives the power to love as God loves. Resting in God's heart, he experiences the pathways of life that will lead him to become the person that God wills for him to be. Anyone whose life resonates with God's word will experience the joy that God wants him to have. This is an important part of what it means to choose life.

Every day you and I are faced with choices that can lead either toward or away from life. God not only invites us to choose life, he also gives us the power to make the right choices. Our part in this process is to know what the right choices are. We do this by reflecting on God's word to see how it applies to ourselves in our everyday lives. This is what we have tried to do as we reflected on the various pathways that can lead us to joy.

It seems to me that prayer will always be an indispensable part of the process. As we spend time with God and reflect on his word, we come to know what is in his heart. We come to see more clearly which choices lead to life, and which ones do not. The more we are in a reflective, loving relationship with God, the more likely it is that our choices will be truly life-giving. This same principle can be experienced in our friendships. The more a person becomes one with his friend, the more he sees how to relate to her in ways that will give life to the friendship.

Our task, then, is to choose life over and over again each day by living according to the designs of God's heart, deepening our relationships with God and with each other in ways that will bring us joy. Our daily choices for life will prepare us for the final choice of eternal life that we will make at the time of our death. This life is a preparation for the one to come, and all the good we do in this life will have its echo throughout eternity.

Choose life! Here is a choice that will bear its ultimate fruit as it leads us to the fullness of resurrected life with Jesus. Are your daily choices as life-giving as you want them to be?

101.

GAZING INTO GOD'S OPEN HEART, WE HAVE BECOME HIS FRIENDS.

"I do not call you servants any longer, because a servant does not know what his master is doing. Instead, I call you friends, because I have told you everything I heard from my Father."

John 15:15

It seems that you could think of this pathway as one that contains all the others, because it is a summary of all that we have considered throughout this book. Jesus has allowed us to gaze deeply into the heart of his Father by revealing to us all that he has seen there. Jesus' words and actions reveal multiple pathways that lead into the life of God. We have seen some of these pathways, and if we travel over them, we gradually evolve into the persons whom God created us to be.

Gazing into God's open heart, we continue to see his thoughts. He has revealed them to us as an act of love that makes us to be his friends. We only reveal ourselves to those whom we consider to be our friends, and so the fact of God's revelation to us tells us something important about ourselves. But we are also his friends through the power of his presence, which always resides within us. Without this enabling presence of God, we would not have the strength to live according to the words he has revealed.

Friends enhance one another's lives. God certainly enhances ours, although the word "enhance" is too weak to describe adequately what God does for us. Of course, no word ever could do that. Perhaps the best we can say is that we live and move and have our being in God. That is the ultimate basis of every good thing that ever happens in our lives. God gives us our being and works with us to bring us to perfection in him. So, yes, God is our friend. And yet even that word can only scratch the surface of what we try to say about our relationship with God.

If we love God, we will continue to walk down the pathways that his word and actions have mapped out for us. All of the pathways lead us to a deeper experience of meaning and joy. God's word only bears its fruit when it is lived and experienced, when it helps us to enter into his presence. We are meant to go beyond the word to experience the heart of God from which it came. The word always points to the heart. When we arrive there, in a loving, trusting union with God, then his word will have born its ultimate fruit in us.

May God's word bear its ultimate fruit in you! Amen.

INDEX

Numbers refer to chapter headings, not to pages.